Common Knit and Crochet Abbreviations

Abbreviation...	What It Means...
1 sc dec	Single-crochet decrease
alt	alternate
approx	Approximately
beg	Begin(ing)
bet	Between
blk	Block
blo	Back loop only
bo	Bind off
bpdc	Back post double crochet
c2b	Cable 2 back
c2f	Cable 2 front
c4b	Cable 4 back
c4f	Cable 4 front
cc	Contrasting color
ch st	Chain stitch
ch	Chain
cn	Cable needle
col	Color
cont	Continue(ing)
dbl	Double
dc	Double crochet
dec 1 dc	Double-crochet decrease
dec	Decrease(ing)
dpn	Double-pointed needle
fin	Finished
foll	Following
fpdc	Front post double crochet
g or gr	Gram(s)
hdc	Half-double crochet
in(s)	Inch(es)
inc	Increase(ing)
k	Knit
k2Tog	Knit 2 together
kbl	Knit through back of loop
kwise	Knit-wise
lp(s)	Loop(s)
m1	Make 1
mc	Main color
med	Medium
mm	Millimeter
mult	Multiple

Abbreviation...	What It Means...
opp	Opposite
oz	Ounces
p tbl	Purl through back of loop
p	Purl
p2tog	Purl two together
pat(s)	Pattern(s)
pc st	Popcorn stitch
pc	Picot crochet
pm	Place marker
psso	Pass slip stitch over
pwise	Purlwise
rem	Remaining
rep	Repeat
rev st st	Reverse stockinette stitch
rib	Ribbing
rnd(s)	Round(s)
rs	Right side
sc	Single crochet
sk	Skip
sl st	Slip stitch
sl	Slip
sp(s)	Space(s)
ssk	Slip slip knit
st st	Stockinette stitch
st(s)	Stitch (es)
tbl	Through back of loop
tog	Together
tr	Triple
trc	Triple crochet
ws	Wrong side
wyib	With yarn in back
wyif	With yarn in front
yb	Yarn back
yf	Yarn forward
yo	Yarn over
ytb	Yarn to back
ytf	Yarn to front

alpha
books

Knitting Needle Conversion Chart

CHART OF INTERNATIONAL NEEDLE EQUIVALENTS														
U.S.	0	1	2	3	4	5	6	7	8	9	10	10 1/2	11	13	15
English/U.K.	13	12	11	10	9	8	7	6	5	4	3	2	1	00	000
Continental Rim	2 1/4	2 1/2	3	3 1/4	3 1/2	4	4 1/2	5	5 1/2	6	6 1/2	7	7 1/2	8 1/2	9

Steel Crochet Hook Conversion Chart

U.S.	1	2	3	4	5	6	7	8	9	10	11	12	13	14
English	3/0	2/0	1/0	1	1 1/2	2	2 1/2	3	4	5	5 1/2	6	6 1/2	7
Continental Rim	3	2.5		2		1.75	1.5	1.25	1	0.75		0.6		

Aluminum and Plastic Crochet Hook Conversion Chart

U.S.	1/B	2/C	3/D	4/E	5/F	6/G	8/H	9/I	10/J	10 1/2 /K
English	12	11	10	9	8	7	6	5	4	2
Continental Rim	2 1/2	3		3 1/2	4	4 1/2	5	5 1/2	6	7

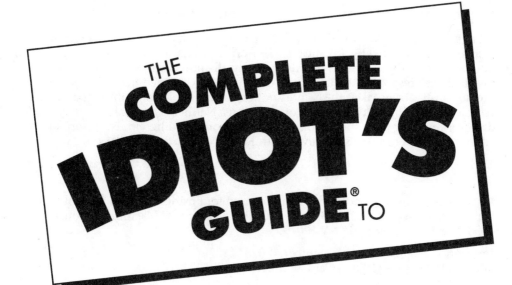

THE COMPLETE IDIOT'S GUIDE® TO

Knitting and Crocheting

By Gail Diven and Cindy Kitchel

alpha books

A Division of Macmillan General Reference
A Pearson Education Macmillan Company
1633 Broadway, New York, NY 10019

Macmillan Publishing books may be purchased for business or sales promotional use. For information please write: Special Markets Department, Macmillan Publishing USA, 1633 Broadway, New York, NY 10019.

International Standard Book Number: 0-02862123-9
Library of Congress Catalog Card Number: 98-89952

01 00 99   3 2 1

Interpretation of the printing code: the rightmost number of the first series of numbers is the year of the book's printing; the rightmost number of the second series of numbers is the number of the book's printing. For example, a printing code of 99-1 shows that the first printing occurred in 1999.

Printed in the United States of America

Alpha Development Team

Publisher
Kathy Nebenhaus

Editorial Director
Gary M. Krebs

Managing Editor
Bob Shuman

Marketing Brand Manager
Felice Primeau

Editor
Jessica Faust

Development Editors
Phil Kitchel
Amy Zavatto

Production Team

Development Editor
Amy Zavatto

Production Editor
Linda Seifert

Cover Designer
Mike Freeland

Illustrators
John Bergdahl
Adam Hurwitz
Jody P. Schaeffer

Designer
Nathan Clement

Indexer
Sandra Henselmeier

Layout/Proofreading
Angela Calvert
Mary Hunt
Julie Trippetti

Contents at a Glance

Contents

Foreword

"Stop knitting," my husband implored as he drove around the nightmare of construction and traffic just outside Chicago. "Your yarn is driving me mad," he continued as he flicked little specks of lilac chenille yarn from in front of his vision. "How can I?" I answered, "five of these sweaters have to be finished by Christmas, in time for Coleen's wedding." My needles had been going constantly on our trip from Iowa to Michigan to visit our son for the annual October parent's weekend. I'd made the grand gesture to create five pastel sweaters of the most delightful French yarn for this lovely girl's sisters to wear atop antique white flowing skirts. "If you don't stop we will both come down with lilac lung disease," complained my Iowa husband. I put down my needles in the interest of our health and well-being.

I had never really attempted anything quite so ambitious in all the years of needlecrafts, since my dear grandmother had started me crocheting afghan squares for the ladies at the Methodist home. Every yarn scrap we had was turned into these little masterpieces that fell from my hook like so many autumn leaves. My squares were better than my sister's, so what further motivation did I need to make knitting and crocheting an important part of my life? My achiever blood ran high. Finding a penchant for knitting in particular, I progressed to hats and mittens.

No self-imposed knitting assignment was as cheerfully taken on as when I decided to make a wardrobe for my first child. Certain I would have a little girl, I turned my attention to very complicated patterns—one woven with ribbons in a particularly feminine shade of lilac. I had a bouncing baby boy, and his father, beginning his attack on lilac, would not allow me to dress him, even once, in the long coat and bonnet I had made for him. He *did* come home from the hospital in a fluffy white bunting of knit and purl and a soft yellow sweater and cap.

My love for needlecrafts didn't stop when my children outgrew the tiny outfits I made for them. I even love to knit during movies, and obtained some wonderful English knitting needles that allow me to silently move from row to row without disturbing my fellow moviegoers. Once, my needles were taken away from me before boarding an airplane. (Would I use these pointed objects in some knitter-gone-mad scheme? I pouted, to say the least.)

Knitting got me through high school—I bonded and became fast friends with the girls who were not yet ready for weekend dates in my freshman year. Even when dates and boyfriends became a regular part of my life, my knitting certainly didn't take the back burner. In college, I moved on to creating socks and sweaters for boyfriends up and down the eastern seaboard. When I got my first job in publishing in New York, I made suits, dresses, and coats and got my office mates to take up knitting as well. Later, I landed a job at a large magazine due to my knitting knowledge, and was to give millions such instructions as a crafts editor.

I hope, through the pages of this book, *The Complete Idiot's Guide to Knitting and Crocheting*, that you too will discover a passion for the time-honored traditions of knitting and crocheting. Authors Gail Diven and Cindy Kitchel give you all the basics, and then help you to put your new skills to work in easy-to-follow instructions that should have you snuggled under a self-made blanket in no time!

I've knitted for me, for loved ones, for work, and for the belief that idle hands are just not such a good thing. Knitting has been useful in so many ways, granting me permission to be peaceful may be the most important. Since that trip to Chicago, though, knitting in the car is still a no-no. Maybe I'll soften my husband up with a new sweater....

May you never drop a stitch,

Nancy Lindemeyer
Editor-in-Chief of *Victoria* magazine

Introduction

Knitting and crocheting have changed significantly in the past couple hundred years. Like many crafts, these two grew out of necessity: People needed a way to take simple tools and supplies and craft them into usable items. Today, base survival barely figures into knitting and crocheting. Your family members aren't dependent on your knitting skills to keep their feet toasty; usable socks are easy enough to buy from a store.

And yet, more and more people continue to learn these crafts. In fact, their popularity has escalated substantially in recent years. Young adults looking for a creative, relaxing outlet are turning to knitting and crocheting as an after-hours escape from life's hectic pace. The choice to stitch or not to stitch adds a new freedom to the crafts that wasn't there either at the turn of the century, when women felt compelled to stitch for survival, or in the liberated '60s, when women felt compelled to make a statement and not stitch. Folks are now knitting and crocheting because they *choose* to.

Over the years I've taught many people—men, women, and children—to knit and crochet. Often when trying to recommend a good beginning-level book as a reference, however, I've come up dry. Some books assume a certain level of knowledge; others don't provide any projects with which to try new skills. Still others are organized so that you must read hundreds of pages of information before trying the few projects at the back of the book.

The Complete Idiot's Guide® to Knitting and Crocheting is different. In this book you'll find a step-by-step approach to mastering basic knitting and crocheting. You'll learn how simple these crafts really are to execute. And, as you add more skills to your repertoire, you'll get a chance to try those skills on real pieces that you'll use again and again.

How to Use This Book

As you'll learn, knitting and crocheting, no matter how exquisite the piece being made, involve only a handful of skills. Once you get the basics under your belt, you can embellish and combine those skills in new ways to create eye-popping usable art.

This book is set up so that you will learn the basics, first of knitting and then of crocheting. As you learn new techniques, you can test them using the projects interspersed throughout the book.

Part 1: Begin at the Beginning, gives you a brief overview of knitting and crocheting as a whole. This part also covers two very important concepts applicable to both crafts: choosing yarn and checking gauge.

Part 2: Knitting Basics, takes you through beginning-level skills. You'll learn to cast on stitches, knit, purl, play with some knit/purl combinations, and bind off the stitches to finish your work. Because you'll no doubt be itching to try your new talents, you'll also get to try a simple-to-knit checkerboard scarf that looks complex but is actually very easy to make and a useable and attractive cotton dishcloth, as well.

Part 3: Taking the Next Step: More Complex Knitting, goes beyond the basics and walks you through some more advanced topics: shaping your work, adding color, knitting seamless tubes, and reading complex knitting patterns. Because you often understand concepts by reinforcing your reading with doing, you'll also get a chance to try your hand at working in color and knitting in circles with a fun roll-brim hat.

Part 4: Crochet Basics, walks you through all the skills you'll need to begin crocheting fabulous pieces. You'll learn to make a foundation chain; single, half-double, double, and triple crochet; increase and decrease stitches; use color; and add decorative touches. With the skills you learn in this part, you'll be able to create fabulous, complex crocheted pieces simply by manipulating and combining the basic stitches. You'll get to work on two impressive but simple projects in this part: a thick and cozy afghan, and a set of plaid placemats.

Part 5: Final Helps, covers topics applicable to knitting and crocheting. First, you'll learn the finishing skills such as seaming and blocking. The book ends with some final thoughts about giving away your hard work: when to do it, what to give, and when to give to yourself.

Extras

This book features a number of valuable sidebars that provide additional information about knitting and crocheting: definitions, historical anecdotes, pitfalls to avoid, and stitching hints and tips.

Pointers

Is there a better way to do something? Are there variations to the common instructions? Check out the Pointers, where you'll learn valuable hints and tips to make your stitching more enjoyable.

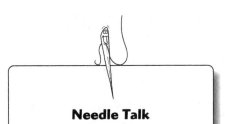

Needle Talk

So many definitions are thrown around in the stitching world: gauge, dye lot, half-double crochet... Look to the Needle Talk notes for simple definitions.

Yarn Spinning

Knitting and crocheting have enjoyed long histories filled with interesting anecdotes. You'll read some of these compelling stories in the Yarn Spinning notes.

Snarls

Danger! Warning! You potentially could hit a bump in the road if you don't watch out for these common errors!

Acknowledgments

This book is the result of the effort and professionalism of a stellar team of people. Thanks to Amy Zavatto and Linda Seifert for their exacting editing, John Bergdahl and Adam Hurwitz for their exceptional illustrations, and the production team at Macmillan: Angela Calvert, Mary Hunt, and Julie Trippetti.

Special Thanks to the Technical Review

The Complete Idiot's Guide® to Knitting and Crocheting was reviewed by an expert who double-checked the accuracy of what you'll learn here to help us ensure that this book gives you everything you need to know about knitting and crocheting.

Hats off to Kate, Katie, Kitty, and Kris, also known as DKG. Our weekly stitching sessions contributed greatly to the content of this book. I learned so much from all of you.

Thanks and love to my parents, Don and Eleanore Morrow, who have always been encouraging of everything I attempt.

Much love to my wonderful husband Phil, who good-naturedly puts up with my compulsive stitching and stashing.

All my love to Edith Lansbury Wilson (1902–1985), who displayed the patience of Job in teaching a six-year-old to knit.

And special thanks to Mark McGwire, Sammy Sosa, and the New York Yankees, who brought joy back to baseball.

—CK

Part 1
Begin at the Beginning

As with any new hobby you pursue, if you learn a few key concepts before plunging in, your start will be much smoother. Knitting and crocheting are no exception.

In the chapters that follow, you'll get a base for your new craft; you'll learn a bit about knitting and crocheting, how to choose yarn, and how to measure gauge. By the time you finish this section, you'll be ready to start stitching.

Chapter 1

Knitting and Crocheting Come Out of Your Grandma's Attic

In This Chapter

➤ The modern popularity of knitting and crocheting

➤ Why learn these skills?

➤ The core concept of knitting and crocheting

Knitting? Crocheting? Didn't those skills go out of vogue with candle-dipping, soap-making, and butter-churning? Absolutely not. True, knitting and crocheting are no longer necessary to life as they were in your grandma's or great-grandma's time. Also true is the fact that the popularity of individual crafts seems to wax and wane with the public's attention span. And yet, knitting and crocheting continue to enjoy popularity. Why, you may ask? They're classics. Like a good Shakespeare play or a Frank Sinatra album, they never go out of style. (And, they sometimes keep you warm, too!)

In this chapter, you'll discover why knitting and crocheting continue to be popular despite no longer being necessary to daily life, why—if you haven't already decided to do so—you might want to become a stitcher, and what lies at the base of these crafts.

Man versus Machine: The Death of Knitting and Crocheting?

Browse through any antique store and you'll find piles of vintage knitted and crocheted whatnots. Knitting and crocheting have been around nearly as long as people have felt the need for clothes and blankets and, consequently, the need to make those items attractive. Chances are, your grandma or great-grandma can hardly remember learning the crafts; before the advent of television, and even radio, knitting and crocheting, for young girls, were skills as fundamental as breathing. These crafts were practiced not only for practical and ornamental reasons, but to entertain as well.

Yarn Spinning

Knitting and crocheting seem to have skipped a generation. These crafts were tremendously popular with those born in the 1920s and 1930s, but experienced a sharp drop with the next generation. Today, one of the stronger age groups of participants are people in the 20- to 30-year-old range. Theories are that the first generation of women who didn't need to knit or crochet to clothe their families and homes chose not to. This generation's sons and daughters, however, have found knitting and crocheting to be a source of relaxation, creativity, and fulfillment.

As mechanism increased, however, the *need* for knitting and crocheting in modern countries has all but disappeared. For instance, while soldiers in the American Revolution, the Civil War, World War I, and World War II all relied on the efforts of home knitters to keep them warm on the battlefield, modern-day soldiers get most of their warm accessories from factories. Even fancy crocheted lace items such as doilies, bedspreads, and tablecloths—once the sole property of the hand crocheter—are now easily produced by machine and sold in local department stores.

You would think the automation that made these crafts unnecessary would have also deemed them extinct. Not so. Knitting and crocheting are ironically gaining in popularity, continuing to enlist thousands of new enthusiasts. In addition, technology has enhanced, rather than hurt, the crafts. One online knitlist, for example, enables Internet users to receive messages, advice, and knitting news from fellow artisans. The list currently has more than 2,000 subscribers, and new subscribers are warned to expect as many as 90 messages per day.

Clearly, knitting and crochet are staying put. And with the help of this book, you'll be able to get in on the fun, too.

Why Bother?

What's the point? If you can walk into a J. Crew at any mall across America and buy a bulky wool sweater, why spend valuable free time knitting and crocheting? By picking up this book you no doubt believe, on some level, that pursuing this endeavor is worthwhile. But if you need a bit more fuel for the proverbial fire, think about these reasons.

Get Creative!

Knitting and crocheting are an art—generally a wearable or usable art, but still an art. When you knit or crochet, you are creating a piece. You are choosing the dimensions; you're changing the look by using novelty yarn or funky colors. You're choosing how you want the finished product to look, and then executing the design. When you purchase a sweater or some other such item, you're not really sure how this item came into existence. Think about cozying up to a beautiful hat or scarf that you made yourself). When a friend asks you where you got these beautiful woolens, you have the rare opportunity to say, "I made it."

And not only do you get to feel the enormous sense of pride and accomplishment in completing such a task—there are other benefits, too. Some experts believe that working with your hands, following repetitive motions—such as those in knitting, crocheting, and needlepoint—actually fuel the creative process in other areas of your life. Julia Cameron, author of *The Artist's Way*, believes that by allowing your hands to work repetitiously, your brain can simultaneously think through solutions creatively. If, for example, you are a writer suffering from seemingly incurable writer's block, the repetitive process of crocheting a few inches of an afghan might enable you to free your mind and work through a plot problem in your latest short story. Or maybe you don't fancy yourself the creative type, but need to find a solution to a problem at work. Stitching can free your mind to find creative life solutions, as well. Quite simply, it's a wonderful outlet for your overworked brain!

Yarn Spinning

Knitting dates very early in the history of man. Actual fragments can only be traced to 200 AD, but these fragments show great sophistication and understanding of the craft, causing historians to believe that the craft originated much earlier.

Make Pieces for Life

Have you noticed that crafts go through phases? One year everyone's making baskets out of crepe paper. The next they're making decoupage planters. Where do most of these items end up? In the basement under the gravity boots? In a yard sale? In a landfill? Sadly, many crafts are built more for speed and fad than for longevity.

On the other hand, if you knit a classic sweater or crochet a beautiful table cover, you've got a friend for life. Once you learn these crafts, you're creating heirlooms.

Snarls

If your stitching time is precious and you want to use the items you knit or crochet for life, try to stick with classic colors, shapes, and fibers. Beware of up-to-the-minute patterns that will be out of vogue in a year or two. A super-trendy piece, whether bought at the mall or labored over for two months, will still look outlandish and out of date in a short period.

Slow Down Your Hectic Pace

While you can fax patterns to friends or hop on the Internet for some help when you get stuck, knitting and crocheting still force you to sit down, slow down, and enjoy the craft. In a world filled with cell phones, beepers, Internet cafes, and video TVs, escaping for an hour to knit a sock heel can be incredibly rejuvenating.

Be forewarned: If you're a Type A personality trying to unwind through knitting or crocheting, you'll have to take special care not to become a Type A stitcher. It's easy to see knitting and crocheting as another thing on your to-do list: *Clean gutters, E-mail quotes to Johnson regarding the housing deal, Knit left sleeve of sweater....* If you find yourself getting too uncomfortably regimented about your knitting and crocheting, put your projects away for a couple days so that taking them out again truly is a treat.

Pointers

In a fit of super-organization, I once made a spreadsheet of unfinished projects. I assigned each project a number of points from 25 (for a washcloth) to 500 (for a multicolor designer cardigan). My goal was to have no more than 1,000 points going at any one time, and to organize which projects would be finished in which week. The system worked for about 2 hours before I felt oppressed. Now if I don't want to face an unfinished project, I throw it in the closet until I feel like working on it again. Never let knitting and crocheting become a task.

Have Crocheting, Will Travel

Knitting and crocheting are both fabulous projects to take on the go. Unlike other hobbies—astronomy, say, or weaving—these crafts can easily be thrown in a bag and pulled out as time allows.

Heading on a family vacation where you'll spend 10 hours in the car on the way to Disneyland? Going to the airport to wait for a plane? Riding the train into the office? Take your knitting and crocheting. A simple project that you can turn to in a traffic jam works wonders on your psyche and makes you feel you've accomplished something in an impotent situation.

Pointers

Treat yourself to a nice bag that lets you carry your projects in style. Don't feel compelled to buy your bag at a crafts store—truthfully, some bags made expressly for knitting or crocheting can be the most hideous things you can carry. Instead, check out a sleek leather backpack at a hiking store, or a gatemouth gardening bag from a home-improvement shop. Keep this bag stocked with a measuring tape, a yarn needle, and some pins, add your current project, and you're ready to go!

You're in Good Company

Many famous people have picked up a crochet hook or knitting needle in their day. In fact, the list of famous knitters and crocheters past and present would require a book all its own. Here's a sampling: Dorothy Parker, Julia Roberts, Isak Dineson, Kaffe Fassett, Eleanor Roosevelt, Martha Washington, Meryl Streep, Lillian Hellman, Cameron Diaz, Vanna White, and the nameless protagonist in Daphne de Maurier's *Rebecca*.

So What, Exactly, Is Knitting and Crocheting?

Glad you asked.

In the next several chapters you're going to learn all about these crafts. You'll learn what tools are necessary, how to prepare to start stitching, how to work the basic stitches, and how to end your work. You'll also learn about adding color and texture, changing the shape of your work, and putting it all together by sewing seams.

Yet, with all these skills, knitting and crocheting involve one simple concept:

> *Knitting and crocheting are simply a means of creating fabric by interlocking loops.*

That's it.

Yarn Spinning

Knitting has undergone a gender change. It started out as a craft mainly pursued by men. Sailors and traders from Arabia were instrumental in passing on this knowledge to the rest of world. It remained predominately a man's craft for centuries. Today, although many men are now accomplished knitters, a greater number of women than men knit.

When you knit, you keep a whole row of loops "active." You use one knitting needle to hold the active loops, or stitches, and another to work the new row of loops.

Pointers

As you get comfortable knitting and crocheting, you'll find that it's the perfect accompanying craft for watching movies. An informal poll of several knitters and crocheters revealed that the following films are exceptional rentals when you want to spend a quiet evening stitching. All these films are dialog-heavy so that you can look down often at your hands: *Breakfast at Tiffany's, Rebecca, The Philadelphia Story, The Usual Suspects, Swing Kids, Twelve Angry Men, Dangerous Liaisons, Manhattan Murder Mystery,* and *A Place in the Sun.*

When you crochet, you keep only one loop at a time active; each stitch seals off the last loop. This means that you need a shorter tool—one that allows you to catch that next loop and pull it through the closed loop on the preceding row. This tool is a crochet hook.

As you learn new concepts in this book, keep reminding yourself *I am simply making loops*. As you work through the steps in this book, notice what your hands are doing. You'll see that every step you make is a means of making and manipulating loops. Knitting and crocheting is not intimidating if you understand the basic concept behind your work.

Are you ready to begin? The next two chapters cover concepts universal to knitting and crocheting: choosing yarn and checking gauge. After that, you'll jump into actual knitting and crocheting, learn the basic concepts and skills, and make some fun projects along the way.

The Least You Need to Know

➤ Despite the machine age eliminating the need for hand-stitched items, the popularity of knitting and crocheting continues.

➤ These crafts can help you slow down a hectic life, flex your creative muscles, and create heirlooms in the bargain.

➤ At their core, knitting and crocheting involve making loops.

Chapter 2

Choose Your Poison: A Yarn Primer

In This Chapter

➤ Put up your yarn: Common packaging

➤ The right thickness for the right job

➤ Selecting a fiber

➤ Gleaning valuable information from yarn labels

➤ Determining how much yarn to buy

➤ Choosing yarns that fit into your budget

All you need to knit or crochet is a needle and some string or yarn. That's it. This chapter helps you wade through the mind-boggling number of yarn choices available and helps you determine exactly what type of yarn meets your needs for different projects.

Once you have a good grasp of what is available to you, you have an infinite number of project possibilities. Start with this yarn primer, look through knitting and crocheting magazines (see Appendix A for resources), and get to work creating a one-of-a-kind piece!

Put Up Your Yarn: Common Yarn Packaging

Walk into a crafts store and you'll be overwhelmed with the vast array of yarn and thread choices available for knitting and crocheting. Most of what you'll see, however, is packaged—or "put up"—in one of four common ways.

Common yarn packaging: ball, skein, hank, and cone.

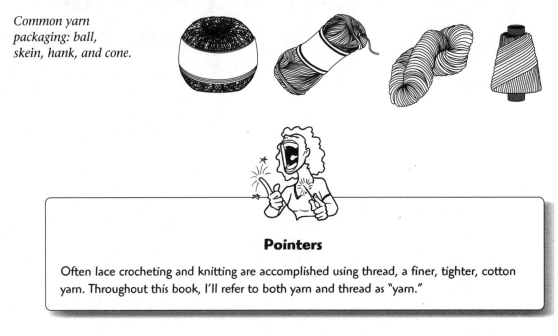

Pointers

Often lace crocheting and knitting are accomplished using thread, a finer, tighter, cotton yarn. Throughout this book, I'll refer to both yarn and thread as "yarn."

Yarn Spinning

Some artists specializing in knitting or crocheting have made their reputations by the unusual "yarn" they choose to manipulate into loops. One example is Katherine Cobey, a Maine-based artist who gained reknown for knitting a wedding gown from strips of white garbage bags.

Here's a short explanation of each type of packaging:

Ball. A ball is exactly what you would expect. Yarn is wound into a ball-like shape, and often the yarn can be pulled from the center of the ball. Cotton crochet thread is almost always packaged in balls.

Skein. A skein is a clever machine-wound bundle of yarn that enables you to pull the yarn from the center. Most synthetic-fiber yarn and many commercial wool or cotton yarns are packaged in skeins.

Hank. A hank is a big circle of yarn twisted into a neater package. To knit or crochet a hank of yarn, you have to untwist the yarn and wind it into a ball. Remember all those Ma and Pa Kettle movies in which a man sat on the porch holding yarn across his forearms while a woman wound it into a ball? That yarn came from a hank. If you don't have a friend available to hold the yarn, you can always drape the big circle over your knees, over the back of a chair, or over a doorknob.

Cone. Cones are commercial put-ups of yarn that often come in one-pound or greater quantities. Purchasing cones of yarn—if you have a good source—is an excellent option. The yarn is often sold by the pound cheaper than comparible amounts in a skein, hank, or ball, and you rarely have to deal with running out of yarn—and having to start up using another skein when you run out of yarn—midway through a project.

> **Needle Talk**
>
> A *yarn winder* is a funky, two-piece contraption that enables you to easily wind skeins of yarn into balls. You secure one piece to one end of a table; secure a second piece to the other end of the table; fit the skein onto the first piece; crank the handle; and wind the yarn from one piece to the other. Sound complex? For now, use a doorknob.

Watching Your Weight: Choosing the Right Thickness for the Right Job

Yarns are categorized according to weight or thickness. Weighted from very fine to bulky, different thicknesses are suitable for different jobs. This section will help you sort out your options.

> **Pointers**
>
> This section provides suggestions for which yarns to use for which projects. Remember, however, that these are suggestions. You control everything about your knitted and crocheted masterpieces, and you can break out of the guidelines any time you want!

Threads

Cotton thread is generally used for crochet projects, although many knitting projects also call for this material. The thread varies from gossamer to bulky weight. Thread differs from yarn mainly in its structure. Thread is twisted much more tightly than yarn and, consequently, has less give than yarn. As a result, cotton thread is an exceptional choice for doilies, placemats, bedspreads, lace edgings, and other projects that require a piece to tautly keep its shape and firmness.

Cotton threads are sized according to numbers. The higher the number, the finer the thread. Numbers start with size 3 and go up to 100. The most common weight is bedspread weight, which is generally a 10-weight size.

Some manufacturers give their cotton thread names instead of numbers, but the label of the product usually describes the type of projects that are suitable for that particular weight.

Yarns

Although many people choose to work with cotton thread, the overwhelming majority of knitters and crocheters choose yarn. The most often-used size is *worsted weight*, but this is certainly not the only choice available.

Yarn is sized according to weight, or the thickness of a single strand. The range goes from fingering weight to bulky. The classifications listed below start with the thinnest and go up to the thickest:

Here's a rundown of available yarn choices:

Fingering weight or baby weight. This thin yarn is well-suited to sweaters with intricate color patterns (such as traditional Fair Isle sweaters), light-weight gloves, airy shawls, baby clothes, and fine-weight socks.

Sport weight. Another popular weight of yarn, this is about twice as thick as fingering weight. Use it for gloves, socks, baby clothes, light-weight sweaters, and shawls.

Double-knitting (DK) weight. This yarn is a smidge thicker than sport weight and a mite thinner than worsted weight. You can use it for any purpose listed for either of these two other yarns.

Yarn Spinning

When crochet appeared in Middle Europe—Italy, France, Belgium, and England—it was considered a lace-making art. Italy referred to this art as "Orvieto Lace."

Yarn Spinning

As part of the restoration of the 18th-Century Warner House in Portsmouth, New Hampshire, 47 volunteers knit an elaborate bedspread to mimic one that had been in the house during the 19th Century. Using tiny needles and miles of cotton thread, the volunteers knit 1,024 squares, which were then pieced together. The project was started in January 1996 and completed in June 1997.

Worsted weight. The most popular thickness of yarn, this weight can be used for nearly any project: mittens, socks, sweaters, afghans—you name it!

Chunky weight. A hefty yarn perfect for hunting sweaters, thick woolen socks, jackets, and afghans.

Bulky weight. The thickest available yarn, bulky is wonderfully warm and thick. Use it for heavy sweaters, jackets, coats, afghans, and pillow covers. Because you can progress incredibly quickly when working with bulky-weight yarn, it's perfect for making impressive last-minute gifts.

Some available yarn thicknesses: double-knitting weight, sport weight, worsted weight, and chunky weight.

Selecting a Fiber

Buying yarn is like buying clothes. Some of us like fluffy fabrics that ooze glamour; others of us find the fibers make us sneeze. Some of us won't go near anything synthetic; others like the easy care acrylics and nylons provide.

Wool yarns. Wool continues to be the most popular choice of knitters and crocheters. Perhaps because it was one of the first materials formed into garments, perhaps because it can create garments that look beautiful for decades, or perhaps because it feels good to work with and keeps its wearer warm. Wool is a wonderful choice for any autumn or winter garment. Afghans are beautiful from wool, but unless made with a superwash variety, can be a bear to clean.

Cotton yarns. Ah, the comfort of cotton. Cotton yarn feels good to work with, wears well, and washes up in the washing machine. On the downside, cotton stretches out of shape more easily than wool, often fades with washing, and has less "tug" on needles than wool, so stitches can get dropped off the needle when knitting.

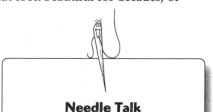

Needle Talk

Superwash wool is wool specially treated to be machine washed and dried without incident. Superwash is a wonderful choice for knitting baby clothes: You get the warmth and comfort of wool without troubling a new mother with time-consuming fabric care.

Pointers

If you're a fairly inexperienced knitter working with cotton, use wooden needles. The needles hold onto slick cotton yarn more easily than do metal ones.

Synthetic yarns. Synthetics aren't what they used to be. Many are beautiful, affordable, vibrant, and attractive—and they require little care and don't attract pests. Synthetic yarns such as acrylic are exceptional for afghans and baby clothes—items that are difficult or very inconvenient to wash by hand. On the other hand, some synthetics pill and can look cheap. As a rule of thumb—if you're making an heirloom, use wool. If you're making a good, solid item to last for a few years, go with synthetics.

Longhaired yarns. If you've seen an Ed Wood movie, you're familiar with angora and its cousin, mohair. Both are beautiful yarns that feature long "hairs" to make the knitted or crocheted item fuzzy. Generally speaking, mohair is priced around the same as wool; angora is upward of 3 times the price of wool. If you're new to knitting and crocheting, save the longhaired yarn for later; the yarns don't let you clearly see stitches you're forming, which can cause a lot of frustration.

Novelty yarns. Fun, funky yarns—made of both natural and synthetic fibers—are created each year. Some examples are metallic threads, chubby bouclé, and soft chenille. In fact, any fiber—from ribbon to raffia—can be knit or crocheted. Have fun using novelty yarns, but keep in mind how an item is going to be used. If you want to make something that will need frequent laundering, choose a fiber that will allow you this option.

Digging for Clues: Learning to Read Yarn Labels

The label on a package of yarn contains innumerable clues to the yarn's make-up. Familiarize yourself with the information that appears on a yarn label. Everything you want to know is there, from fiber content to dye-lot number.

Take a look at the following list and yarn label. When it comes time to purchase your yarn you will know just what to look for.

```
COLOR NAME/NUMBER
DYE-LOT NUMBER

MANUFACTURE'S NAME
LLL  BRAND
      NAME
LOGO    FIBER CONTENT

YARN SIZE OR PLY

Put-up Weight oz/g
Yarn Length in Yards/Meters

           SUGGESTED GAUGE
8 mm       Needle/Hook Size

CARE INSTRUCTIONS

Manufacture's Address
```

The yarn label speaks volumes about the yarn you're going to purchase.

Let's walk through what each of these items on a yarn label means.

Color Name/Number. The color name and/or number is the name the company has given this color. An example might be: 063067 Sunset Gold.

Dye-Lot Number. The dye-lot number indicates exactly in which dye this yarn was colored. Just as you'll get slight color and tone variations if you use different dye lots when wallpapering your house, you'll get slight but noticeable color variations if you knit or crochet an item using several different dye lots of the same color. Some synthetic yarn doesn't have a dye lot; this information is usually indicated—in bold letters—on the front of the yarn.

Manufacturer's Name. This is the name of the company that made the yarn. For example, Classic Elite or Patons.

Brand Name. The brand name is the name the company assigned this line of yarn. Some examples are La Gran (by Classic Elite) and Chunky (by Patons).

Fiber Content. You guessed it—this is the place where you'll learn what the yarn is made from. Examples are 100% alpaca and 75% cotton/ 25% ramie.

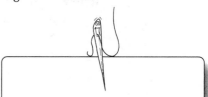

Needle Talk

Dye lot is an indicator of the time the yarn was dyed. Different dye lots—even in the same color yarn— have slight variations in tone. Always check the dye lot (which appears right below the color name and number) and be sure you purchase enough skeins or hanks of yarn in the same dye lot to complete your project.

15

Pointers

Find some yarn in your grandma's workbasket, and you're not sure whether it's wool or synthetic? Try this simple test: Use a match to light the end of the yarn. If it melts together, it's synthetic. If it burns and flakes off, it's wool.

Yarn Size or Ply. This is where you'll learn whether the yarn is a fingering weight, worsted weight, or bulky.

Put-Up Weight. The put-up weight is the actual weight of the skein. In many cases, the yardage is a better indicator of how much yarn the skein contains and how much you'll need to finish a project.

Yarn Length in Yards/Meters. The yarn length is a more accurate indicator than weight of how much yarn the skein contains. Because yards of different fibers weigh differing amounts (cotton, for example, is generally heavier than wool), when you're substituting yarn you'll want to pay special attention to yardage.

Suggested Gauge. You'll learn more about gauge in the next chapter. For now, just know that these small pictures depict what the yarn manufacturer believes will be the gauge (stitches required to make an inch) if you use the size knitting needle or crochet hook shown on the label.

Pointers

Always read the yarn label and follow the manufacturer's advice before you wash or dry clean your finished product. Your time and effort is going into your project, you want the results to last.

Care Instructions. Here's where you get to the meat of the matter: how to care for the yarn. Let's walk through the four symbols you see here in the figure. The first symbol shows that you may wash the wool in 40° Celsius/104° Fahrenheit water; if the symbol had had an × through it, you could not wash it in water. The second symbol indicates that you may wash the wool in a washing machine. The third symbol indicates that you may not bleach the yarn; if this symbol didn't contain an ×, you could bleach. The final symbol shows that the garment may be dry-cleaned using any dry-cleaning solution; if the symbol had an × through it, it could not be dry-cleaned.

How Much to Buy?

Most patterns you use tell you the type yarn suggested (or used for the model) and the number of ounces or number of yards necessary to complete the project. If you use the yarn suggested in the pattern, always buy at least the number of skeins indicated. To be safe, buy one extra. You generally can exchange the extra for other store merchandise or use it for other projects. Nothing's worse than running out of yarn and being unable to get the last bit you need.

In many cases, you'll find that you want to substitute in a different yarn; consequently, you'll need to know how much of the substitute yarn to purchase. Here's how to determine how much yarn you need:

1. If the indicated yarn includes yardage per skein, multiply the number of yards in each ball by the number of skeins required. For example, if each skein contains 100 yards and the pattern requires you to have 9 skeins, you'll need 900 yards (100 yards per skein × 9 skeins = 900 yards).

Pointers

If a pattern includes only the weight (number of ounces) of the yarn but not the yardage, call a local yarn shop and explain that you need the yardage of a specific skein of yarn. Generally, these shops have published resources they can use to track yardage.

2. Find the yardage of each skein of the yarn you want to substitute and divide the number of total yards you need by the number of yards in each skein. For

example, if the yarn you're substituting contains 150 yards per skein, then you'll need 6 skeins. (900 yards needed ÷ 150 yards per skein = 6 skeins.)

Spinning Yarn into Gold

All right, let's get down to reality here. There's all this talk of beautiful angora yarns; captivating, heirloom-creating wools; and fine bleached cotton thread glamorous enough to make a vintage-looking bedspread. No doubt one thought is going through your head: What's all this going to cost me?

Pointers

If you have true budgetary concerns, buy thin yarn. Four ounces of fingering-weight wool can keep you happily knitting for weeks. If price is no object and you love seeing fast results, buy thicker yarn.

As with any hobby, you can spend a lot on yarn (and knitting and crocheting accessories, as you'll learn in Chapters 4 and 16). Or you can be fairly conservative and conscientious.

Keep in mind that price does not always indicate quality. Often solid wool is relatively inexpensive and space-dyed acrylic that pills in the first washing is prohibitively costly. As a rule of thumb, start with a medium-priced wool or cotton in a color and weight that you love.

Needle Talk

A yarn *stash* is the inevitable and seemingly spontaneous ferreting away of pounds and pounds of yarn you don't need but think you might use later. So long as the kids are fed and the bills are paid, never feel guilty about a yarn stash; half the pleasure of knitting and crocheting is enjoying the variety of available fibers.

If you have no idea where to start, walk into a local yarn shop, tell the salesperson you are a beginning knitter and want to spend no more than $10 total for a couple skeins of wool or cotton, and see what happens. If the salesperson is rude and dismissive, don't darken her doors again.

Pointers

Most large chain craft stores such as Michael's and Hobby Lobby will have some wool and cotton at workable prices. Two examples are Sugar 'n Cream cotton, which is generally no more than $1.75 per 2 1/2-ounce skein, and Lion Brand undyed Fisherman's Wool, which is no more than $8.99 per 8-ounce skein.

Here are some ideas for keeping prices down while you are learning to knit or crochet:

Buy cones of yarn. This sounds like a crazy notion—buying in bulk when you're learning a craft—but it's almost always the cheapest way to buy high-quality natural fibers. Two great sources for cones of yarn can be found on the Web: Webs at **www.yarn.com** and School Products at **www.schoolproducts.com**. Webs wool ranges from $8.95 to $23.95 per pound; School Products sells wool at $20 per pound.

Look for close-outs. Like clothing stores, yarn stores need to clear out last-year's colors to make room for this-year's merchandise. Often, you'll find savings of more than 50 percent off the original price by simply frequenting stores fairly often.

Check out thrift stores. Amazingly, some of the best yarn deals around are found in thrift stores. Some knitters have reported finding bags of mohair and wool for less than $2. This avenue is definitely worth a try, and you might find a lava lamp or lawn goose in the meantime.

Put out the word. If you have friends who knit or crochet, they'll probably be thrilled to provide you with some of their leftover skeins from long-ago completed projects.

As with learning any new craft, take it slowly. Don't run out and buy everything you think you may (or may not) need to begin knitting and crocheting. Soon enough you'll have yarn stashed in every available place in your house; don't rush it.

The Least You Need to Know

➤ Yarn options are limitless and exciting; no matter what thickness, fiber, color, or texture you desire, it's available.

➤ The label on yarn provides invaluable information about the yarn you are purchasing, including care information.

➤ Always check the dye lot and make sure you're purchasing all skeins of yarn from a single dye lot.

➤ Knowing the number of yards of yarn required to finish a project is often much more accurate than knowing the number of ounces.

➤ Knitting and crocheting does not have to break the bank; cost-conscious yarn options are available.

Chapter 3

Don't Skip This Chapter! Checking Your Gauge

In This Chapter

➤ What is gauge?

➤ Seeing gauge in items

➤ When to be concerned with gauge

➤ Swatching patterns to determine gauge

➤ Fixing incorrect gauge

What comes to mind when you think of *gauge*? A measure of tire pressure? Pounds per pressure when canning summer tomatoes? The name of the toddler in *Pet Semetary* who killed Fred Gwynne, TV's lovable Herman Munster? It's all these things, but *gauge* is also the most important concept you will learn in knitting and crocheting.

Pardon?

What Is Gauge?

Gauge when knitting or crocheting follows the same concept as gauges used in other practices; it is a measurement of how big or small each of your stitches will be, based on several factors:

➤ The stitch,

➤ how tightly or loosely you knit or crochet,

➤ the yarn, and

➤ the size of the knitting needles or crochet hook.

In addition, your mood can sometimes affect gauge. As you become more accustomed to knitting and crocheting, you might find that the stitches you knit an evening after you've been stuck in a traffic jam for 90 minutes are tighter that those you make while sipping a martini at Martha's Vineyard. Unless you have violent, tumultuous, Jekyl-and-Hyde mood swings, however, the difference between your relaxed knitting and your tense knitting won't be significant enough to worry you.

Can I See Gauge in Action?

Sure you can. Let's start by looking for gauge differences in knitted items.

Are you wearing a T-shirt? Take a look at it. Notice the tiny adjoining loops that make up the fabric? You're looking at a very tight gauge. Now look at a sweater. If it's a bulky J. Crew lime-colored handknit, you'll notice that it still contains loops—just like the T-shirt—but the loops are much larger. This is a much looser gauge. Both items are knitted, but the size of the stitches varies significantly.

Likewise, look at a crocheted doily. Notice a difference in the loop sizes between the doily and the afghan on the back of your couch?

Needle Talk

Gauge is the number of stitches you need to complete to finish a specified length of knitted fabric. Gauge is typically measured by the inch, such as *5 stitches per inch* or *7 stitches per inch.*

Pointers

For a look at some humongous stitches, take a sneak peak at the afghan you'll make in Chapter 18; the stitch size used in this piece is a far cry from antique crocheted lace!

Think about it. If you're using thick needles and thick yarn, it stands to reason that you'll get chunkier stitches.

The following illustration shows two knitted pieces. Both pieces are 20 stitches wide and 15 deep, but one is knit on size 2 needles using baby-weight yarn, while the other is knit on size 11 needles using chunky-weight yarn. You don't need your sleuthing hat to see the obvious differences between these two samples.

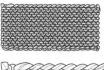

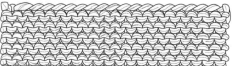

Knitting the same number of stitches using different size needles and different thicknesses of yarn.

How Does Gauge Affect Me?

Suppose that you want to make a beautiful oversized sweater that should be about 44 inches around when complete. You'll need to make sure that the gauge and the number of stitches you work with match the size sweater you want to make. Generally speaking, knitwear designers use the following formula when creating patterns:

> Stitches per inch (*gauge*) × number of inches = number of stitches

Whew. Feel like you're taking a grad-school entrance exam? Hang on. I'll explain.

How Do Patterns Specify Gauge?

Most patterns specify knitting gauge. It might be called something else, such as "stitch measurement" or "tension," but the information is the same. This gauge tells you the number of stitches you make to complete a specified amount of knitted fabric. If your gauge when knitting or crocheting matches the gauge given in the pattern, the item you're making will be the same size as the one indicated in the pattern. If your gauge is off, the finished item will also be off.

Suppose, for example, that a pattern shows the following:

> Gauge: 20 stitches equal 4 inches
> (10 centimeters)

Snarls

Knitting without knowing your gauge is like sailing a boat without a compass. You'll get somewhere, but it might not be where you wanted to go. It's better to take the few extra minutes to make a swatch than to later regret not making one.

Snarls

U.S. needle and hook sizes are different from European and Continental needle and hook sizes. Be sure that the pattern you're reading is specifying the type needle or hook you have. If you need help converting a British pattern to American needles or vice versa, see the tear-out card at the front of this book.

This means the pattern assumes that when you knit or crochet, every 20 stitches you complete will be 4 inches wide in the fabric. If you divide the 20 stitches by 4 (the number of inches), you see that every inch will be 5 stitches:

20 stitches (number of stitches) ÷ 4 (number of inches) = 5 stitches per inch

This is a gauge of 5 stitches per inch.

What Happens If My Gauge Doesn't Match the Pattern?

So what happens if you decide to poo-poo gauge? Let's do a little math. Just a little.

Say you're making a sweater that is to be 44 inches around when finished. That means the front and back each will be 22 inches across (plus a seam, if you have one, but never mind that for now). The pattern specifies that the gauge should be 5 stitches to the inch (20 stitches per 4 inches), and that you should cast on 110 stitches.

Here's why the designer chose 110 stitches:

22 (completed inches) × 5 (stitches per inch) = 110

But what if you work a bit tighter than the pattern specifies? Not much tighter, mind you, but say you knit or crochet about 6 stitches per inch. Now you've got to divide that 110 stitches by 6 and you get a lot fewer inches:

110 (total stitches) ÷ 6 (number of stitches per inch) = $18^1/_3$ inches (completed inches)

If both the front and back of the sweater are $18^1/_3$ inches wide rather than 22 inches, you're going to end up with a 36- to 37- inch, fanny-hugging sweater. Pass the SlimFast.

What if you work a bit looser than the pattern specifies? Not a lot looser, but let's say your actual gauge is 4 stitches per inch rather than the specified 5 stitches per inch. Here's that math again:

110 (total stitches) ÷ 4 (number of stitches per inch) = $27^1/_2$ (completed inches)

If both the front and back of the sweater are $27^1/_2$ inches wide rather than 22 inches, your sweater will be 55 inches around. Prepare to belly up to the Thanksgiving table this year; you've got a lot of fattening up to do.

Yarn Spinning

Many years ago, I knit a sweater for a boyfriend who was only a half-inch taller than me and outweighed me by maybe $1^1/_2$ pounds. I hadn't yet mastered gauge and chose a yarn too thick for the Aran sweater I made. Consequently, my boyfriend looked like a five-year-old playing dress-up. Knitting superstition claims that once you finish an item for a nonspousal significant other, the relationship ends. True to lore, we broke up right after the sweater-dress incident.

As you'll learn later in this chapter, diverting disaster can be as easy as changing the size needle or hook you use.

Is Gauge Ever Unimportant?

Some projects don't have to be so precise, and you can be a bit cavalier with gauge. All of the patterns in this book, except the knitted cap, don't require you to be militant about gauge. These items, if they're a little bigger or a little smaller than the specified size, will still be completely useful and legitimate. (All of the patterns include a gauge, but they also indicate when gauge isn't so important.) In many cases if your gauge is close, you're fine. For example, if you're making any of these items, you don't really need to worry too much about gauge:

➤ Afghans

➤ Pillows that are using stuffing rather than preformed pillow designs

➤ Washcloths and dishcloths

➤ Hot pads

➤ Scarves

➤ Placemats

➤ Unfitted shawls

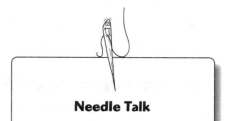

Needle Talk

A *swatch* is a sample you knit or crochet to determine whether your gauge is where it should be.

Checking Your Gauge

Checking your gauge, then, is an essential step when you're knitting or crocheting any item that is size-sensitive. Imagine a pair of socks three times as wide as your ankles. (I don't have to imagine those socks; I have a pair I made out of inappropriately thick yarn.)

To check gauge, you have to knit or crochet a sample, called a swatch, and measure that sample.

To measure your swatch, you can use either a good old-fashioned measuring tape or a commercial gauge counter.

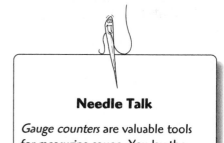

Needle Talk

Gauge counters are valuable tools for measuring gauge. You lay the counter over your knitting or crocheting and count the number of stitches that appear in the window.

Two tools for measuring swatches: A gauge counter and a measuring tape.

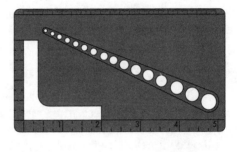

Measuring Gauge When Knitting

To measure gauge when knitting, knit the specified number of inches and rows, and measure them. If the pattern specifies a particular type of stitch to measure (such as, "20 stitches per 4 inches over moss stitch"), knit your swatch using that stitch. Otherwise, use stockinette stitch: Knit one row, purl one row.

Check knitting gauge using either a measuring tape or gauge counter.

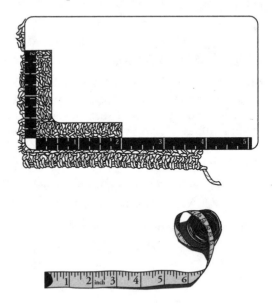

Do you have more stitches per inch than the pattern specifies? Try a larger needle size. Do you have fewer stitches per inch than the pattern requires? Try a smaller needle size. Continue moving up or down one needle size until your swatches match the gauge indicated in the pattern.

Unless you're using a yarn that isn't compatible for what you're trying, the gauge will come out correctly after you fiddle a bit with different needle sizes. If, however, you're trying to use a chunky hand-spun yarn on a pattern that features fine baby yarn, you're probably barking up the wrong tree. Even drastically changing needle sizes can't work those kind of miracles.

Measuring Gauge When Crocheting

To measure gauge when crocheting, crochet the specified number of inches and rows, and measure them. If the pattern specifies a particular type of stitch to measure (such as, "15 stitches per 4 inches over triple shell"), knit your swatch using that stitch. Otherwise, use single crochet.

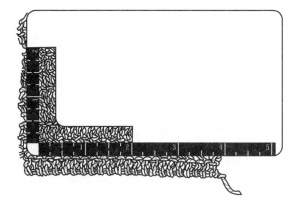

Check crocheting gauge using a gauge counter.

Do you have more stitches per inch than the pattern specifies? Try a larger hook. Do you have fewer stitches per inch than the patter requires? Try a smaller hook. Continue moving up or down one hook size until your swatches match the gauge indicated in the pattern.

The Height's Okay, but the Weight's a Bit Hefty

In some cases, you'll be able to get either the height (20 stitches equals 4 inches) or width (24 rows equal 4 inches) correct, but both won't cooperate at the same time. Let's say 20 stitches equals 4 inches, but 24 rows equals 3³/₄ inches. What to do?

In most cases, you most need to get the width right. Look through the rest of the pattern. Does it tell you to knit or crochet in inches rather than rows, like this:

> Continue knitting until sleeve cap equals 5 inches

If so, just make sure that the width is correct, and you should be fine with the rows. You may, however, need additional yarn—to compensate for the additional rows—to finish the project.

Extra Helps: Searching for Gauge Clues

As you learned in Chapter 2, yarn labels can be bastions of information about everything from fiber content to suggested gauge. Although you'll still need to make a swatch to determine which needle size will give you the correct gauge, the yarn label can be a tremendous help when you're substituting yarn.

If the yarn is a teensy bit off from the gauge specified in your pattern, you can usually fiddle with needle sizes to get the gauge you need. For example, if the yarn label specifies that the gauge is 18 stitches to 4 inches and you need 16 stitches to 4 inches, you can probably use bigger-sized needles and get the correct gauge. If, however, the yarn specifies 20 stitches to 4 inches and you need 12 stitches to 4 inches, pick another yarn.

Switching from Swatching

So what if you just can't face the idea of swatching?

When you're first learning to knit or crochet, fiddling with swatches can be tiresome enough to make you want to give up the hobby. Initially you won't be a speedy stitcher, so creating a four-inch square of fabric that you won't use for anything can be heartbreaking. Make up a few dishcloths and a scarf instead. When you feel comfortable with the process and feel a little quicker and more ready to tackle a bigger project, then dig out a project that will require size to be accurate. As an added bonus, as you get more comfortable knitting and crocheting, your personal gauge will become more regular and predictable.

Pointers

Want to do a little swatching while still making items you can use? Knit up the dishcloth in Chapter 10 using size 8 needles. Then make it with size 10 or size 6 needles. Notice the difference between the finished sizes?

A Final Exhortation

If this all seems like too much work, think of the time it'll take you to knit an item using the wrong gauge, rip out the item, and knit it again. Or think of how heartbreaking it would be to see an ill-fitting item you've tenderly knitted for a loved one stuffed at the bottom of a drawer under the Menudo albums because you didn't check gauge. Checking the gauge is worth every second you spend knitting up swatches. If you just aren't into gauge, stick to knitting items in which gauge isn't important.

Is Gauge Nothing but a Boil on My Neck?

Absolutely not. While making swatches and checking for gauge in patterns might seem like a big pain, knowing the gauge can be incredibly important when you want to break away from a pattern and forge your own path.

Even if all knitters and crocheters were equal and if, provided you used the needle or hook size and yarn type specified, you could be guaranteed that the gauge would be correct and match the pattern precisely, you still want to know how to check gauge. Why?

➤ Suppose you come across a beautiful vintage pattern you want to try but the yarn is no longer available. By using gauge you can determine another yarn to use that will produce the same-sized results.

Pointers

Want to check out some fun, free vintage patterns to test your gauge prowess? Look up Suzu's Glamour Knitting Page on the Web at **http://www.interlog.com/~suzu/s_k_vint.htm.**

➤ What if you find a pattern you love but for which the yarn specified is, in your opinion, frightfully ugly? Or prohibitively expensive? By understanding gauge, you easily can substitute in another yarn. You just need to make sure that the new yarn works up to the gauge in the pattern.

➤ What if you have a gorgeous yarn in your stash that you want to try on a pattern you've found? (We briefly touched on the inevitable stash in Chapter 2.) Stitch up a swatch and see whether the yarn can be used in that pattern.

What Do I Do with All These Little Squares?

While swatches help you determine gauge, they can also serve several other purposes. After you work up a swatch, you can throw it in the washer and dryer to test for shrinkage. You can rub on it a bit to see whether it has a tendency to pill. If you're really feeling saucy, you can pin it to some clothes you're wearing and walk around in it all day, seeing how it wears.

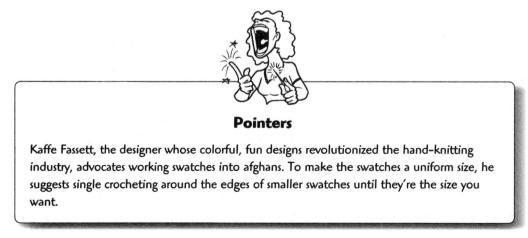

Pointers

Kaffe Fassett, the designer whose colorful, fun designs revolutionized the hand-knitting industry, advocates working swatches into afghans. To make the swatches a uniform size, he suggests single crocheting around the edges of smaller swatches until they're the size you want.

If you're feeling ambitious and you're one of those people who saves drawers full of bread ties because you can't stand being wasteful, you can save all your swatches and later sew them into a crazy-quilt afghan. If you don't have quite enough swatches for a whole afghan, you can make placemats or pillow covers.

The Least You Need to Know

➤ The stitch, yarn type, and needle size determine gauge, as well as how loosely or tightly you knit.

➤ Not all items require gauge to be correct; afghans, pillows, and scarves are safe items to make when you don't feel like dinking with gauge.

➤ To determine gauge, work a swatch of fabric and measure to determine whether the stitches you make per inch match the number specified in the pattern.

➤ To change gauge, change the needle or hook size: higher for a looser gauge, smaller for a tighter gauge.

➤ Always test gauge when making a sweater or other fitted item; you'll save yourself lots of time in the end.

➤ Use the needle or hook sizes indicated in patterns as a guide, but determine the size you should use by working a swatch and measuring gauge.

Part 2
Knitting Basics

You've got the big-picture concepts under your belt. You understand how to choose a yarn and you've been given the proper warnings about not ignoring gauge. What next? Knitting!

This section takes you through the basics of knitting: what tools you do (and don't) need, how to prepare the yarn and hold the needle, how to knit and purl, how to increase and decrease stitches, and how to bring the whole thing to a graceful close. If you're itchin' to get stitchin', you can also try your hand at a couple fun projects.

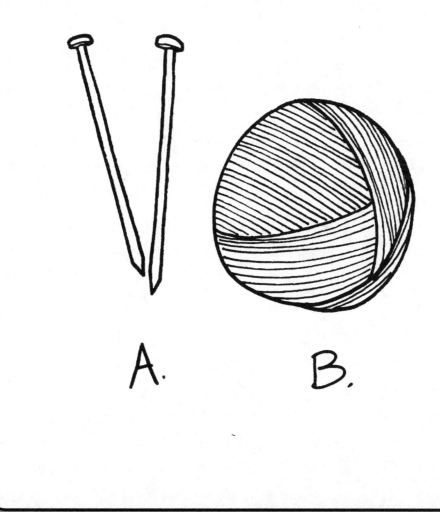

A.　　　B.

Chapter 4

An Overview of Knitting Tools

In This Chapter

➤ Knitting Needles 101

➤ Wading through the needle-sizing muddle

➤ Other accessories that add to your stitching enjoyment

As you begin to explore knitting, the mind-blowing number of accessories might confuse you: Cable needles, stitch markers, yarn bras??

This chapter explains the most common and basic knitting tools—those that make your knitting more enjoyable, more productive, and more beautiful. You don't need to buy each of these tools right away; many you won't need for a long time. You do, however, need to be aware of what's available.

Knitting Needles

Knitting needles are one of only two items necessary for successful knitting—the other item is yarn. Walk into any knitting store, however, and you can easily be overwhelmed and intimidated by the number of options. (Add to this an unhelpful sales person, and you can be scared away from knitting forever.) This section helps you sort out the tangle of needle options.

Straight or Circular?

Knitting needles come in two varieties: straight and circular.

Likewise, straight needles come in two varieties: single pointed and double pointed. Single-pointed needles have a point at one end and a nub or knob at the other; the point is what you knit from and the nub is what keeps stitches from falling off the needle. These needles are sold in pairs and are used for flat knitting, such as scarves. Many sweaters, as well, are knitted in pieces using single-pointed needles. Most cartoon characters you see knitting are using single-pointed needles with nubs. As you'll learn in the next chapter, however, these characters' form is all wrong.

Single-pointed needles are used for knitting flat pieces such as scarves.

Double-pointed straight needles, as you might guess, have points at both ends. Consequently, you can knit from both ends. As you'll learn in Chapter 11, "Knitting in the Round," you generally use these needles to make tubular, seamless items such as socks or mittens. Double-pointed straight needles are sold in sets of four or five needles.

Double-pointed straight needles let you work tubular items like socks and mittens.

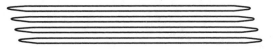

Circular needles create tubes in much the same way as do double-pointed straight needles. Unlike double-pointed needles, however, circular needles enable you to work on one needle only, knitting in a continuous circle. Circular needles have two short single-pointed knitting needles on each end attached by a flexible cord. Circular knitting needles come in sizes ranging from 12" (for socks and mittens) to 36" (for the largest sweaters imaginable).

Pointers

In some cases, if a flat piece such as an afghan has more stitches than will fit on a pair of single-pointed needles, you might use a circular needle to knit back and forth—rather than in a circle—to accommodate all the stitches. In addition, the flexibility of a circular needle means that your work can lay in your lap; you don't have to support its full heft as you would with straight needles.

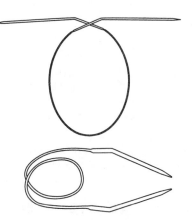

Circular knitting needles enable you to knit in a circle.

Is That American or English?

Knitting needles come in different sizes, and these sizes affect the size of the finished stitch. Easy enough. But going by nothing but a number can get a little tricky because knitting needles can be sized using three different systems: U.S., English/U.K., and Continental Rim. The following chart shows the needle equivalents between these three systems.

CHART OF INTERNATIONAL NEEDLE EQUIVALENTS															
U.S.	0	1	2	3	4	5	6	7	8	9	10	10½	11	13	15
English/U.K.	13	12	11	10	9	8	7	6	5	4	3	2	1	00	000
Continental Rim	2¼	2½	3	3¼	3½	4	4½	5	5½	6	6½	7	7½	8½	9

Trekking Through the Material World

The materials from which knitting needles are made vary considerably. Don't be surprised if you find needles made of

➤ Plastic

➤ Aluminum

➤ Teflon

➤ Wood

➤ Bamboo

➤ Bone

➤ Ivory (although this is extremely rare)

Generally, most needles are made from wood, bamboo, or aluminum. If you don't already have needles and need to buy some, start with a wood or bamboo set. Stitches slide around more on aluminum needles, which can be disconcerting for new knitters. Also, aluminum conducts heat and cold. If you're knitting by a fire, your needles might get hot and uncomfortable to the touch. If you're sitting on the porch on a brisk autumn day, the needles could get cold and uncomfortable to the touch. Wood and bamboo stay at a fairly standard temperature.

Accessories Make the Job Easier

There's a gadget for just about anything you can imagine—and some things you can't. The mail order business has made a fortune selling Ginsu knife sharpeners, turkey-jerky-dehydrating machines, bloomin'-onion devices, and a million other accessories. As you might guess, knitting hasn't escaped this phenomena. Some accessories add little to your knitting experience, but the ones mentioned in this section will prove invaluable as you gain experience.

Snarls

Always check patterns carefully to determine which sizing systems were used. Sometimes, this involves a little creative sleuthing. If, for example, a pattern book was originally printed in England, it very well might use English/U.K. sizing; if it was printed in America, it probably uses U.S. sizing. Often patterns will provide both U.S. and English/U.K. sizing. The patterns in this book are all sized using the U.S. system.

Yarn Spinning

The day he was beheaded in 1649, King Charles (Charles Stuart) wore a shirt made by a master knitter. Today, the shirt is on display at the London Museum.

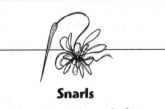

Snarls

A rough point on the end of your needle will snag your yarn when you insert the needle into your stitch. It is very important to have a smooth, sharp—but not deadly—point to stitch properly and comfortably.

Measuring Tools

A good tape measure and gauge counter help you immeasurably (no pun intended) as you begin knitting. You can use both to check knitting gauge, as you learned in Chapter 3. In addition, you can use the tape measure for a million other knitting tasks: measuring the length of a sock from cuff to heel; taking the true waist size of your best friend, to whom you promised a sweater; and so on.

While you can wait to purchase most of the accessories in this section, go out at lunch and buy yourself a good tape measure. You'll be using it almost immediately.

Yarn Spinning

By the 15th and 16th centuries, the art of knitting had become proficient and silk knitting was introduced. The garments knitted at this time were so elaborate, laced with gold and silver threads, that they became garments for the nobility.

Various measuring tools.

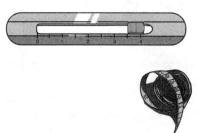

Stitch Holders

Stitch holders are exactly what the name implies: a place to hold stitches that you aren't currently using but will need again. Shaped like big safety pins, stitch holders come in a variety of lengths. In a pinch, if you only need to hold onto a couple of stitches, you can use a safety pin.

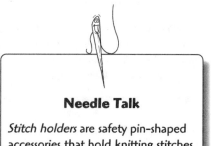

Needle Talk

Stitch holders are safety pin-shaped accessories that hold knitting stitches you aren't currently using but will use later.

A variety of stitch holders in different sizes.

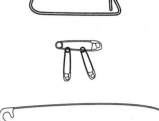

Pointers

If you have a number of stitches you want to hold for working later, you can make your own stitch holder. Thread a strand of contrasting yarn into a yarn needle, and then thread the needle through the stitches you want to hold. Tie the yarn ends together to secure the stitch holder. When you want to use the stitches, cut the contrasting thread and place the stitches back on your needle.

Stitch Markers

Stitch markers are the knitting equivalent of a looped string around your finger: They remind you of important steps in your knitting. These little plastic or metal disks slide onto your needle and cue you to changes in the knitted fabric. You might use them to remind you of which stitch on the row you need to start a cable pattern, or where you need to decrease a stitch.

Stitch markers are available in a variety of shapes; because you need one large enough to slip from needle to needle but not so large as to be obtrusive, you might ultimately need to purchase some in different sizes. In a pinch, you can use a loop of contrasting yarn, a safety pin, or a paper clip as a stitch marker.

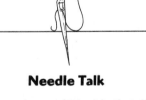

Needle Talk

Stitch markers are little disks that slide onto your knitting needle and cue you at the point when it's time to do something to the knitted fabric.

Stitch markers help you remember important steps in your knitting.

Cable Needles

Look at an Aran-knit sweater and you'll probably be perplexed by the different patterns twisting and swirling up and through the garment. These details are courtesy of cable needles, small, double-pointed needles that hold stitches and help you "move" stitches across a knitting piece. (You'll learn a lot more about cabling and cable needles in Chapter 7.)

The most common shapes are straight, straight with a bend in the middle, and U-shaped. The last two are especially handy as the stitches do not slide off the cable needle. Like regular needles, cable needles are available in a variety of sizes. In a pinch, you can use a regular double-pointed needle or a crochet hook as a cable needle, but these can be more cumbersome and cause you to drop stitches.

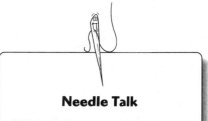

Needle Talk

Cable needles are small double-pointed needles made expressly for creating patterned cables, such as those on Aran sweaters.

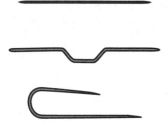

Cable needles enable you to make richly patterned designs.

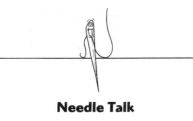

Bobbins help you keep your work from becoming a tangled mess.

Bobbins

Bobbins are helpful accessories to have on hand when you're working in multiple colors. These little gems are made of plastic and are easy to find in yarn shops. Bobbins look similar to bread-bag tabs, only larger. To use a bobbin, wrap yarn around it and knit from the bobbin, rather than from a ball of yarn. You can then unwind only what you need for the next few stitches, and you won't have to negotiate cumbersome amounts of yarn.

Crochet Hooks

"Wait!" You say, "This is the section on knitting." True, but you'll still find yourself thankful for a crochet hook. A crochet hook helps you pick up dropped stitches (which you will learn about in Chapter 15); it enables you to add finishing crochet to the edge of knitted items; it allows you to join seams using a crochet stitch; it lets you attach fringe. You should have at least a few sizes of crochet hooks in your knitting basket. I suggest a steel hook size 0 and an aluminum hook size G.

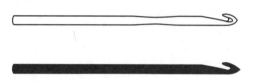

A crochet hook might become your favorite knitting companion.

Needles and Pins

These little helps are irreplaceable when it comes time to finishing your work. You'll use straight pins to block your pieces and hold seams together as you sew or crochet them into place. You'll use yarn needles, which are special needles with dull points and large eyes, to tuck in yarn ends and sew together seams.

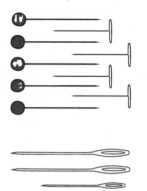

Needles and pins let you bring your work to a graceful close.

The Least You Need to Know

➤ Different varieties of knitting needles enable you to knit either flat or tubular pieces.

➤ Knitting needles come in three varieties—U.S., English/U.K., and Continental Rim—and each uses a different sizing scheme.

➤ A couple of additional accessories such as cable needles and pins will make your life much easier.

Chapter 5

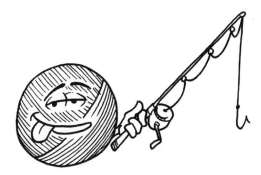

Building the Foundation: Casting On Stitches

In This Chapter

➤ The thumb and cable cast-on methods

➤ Determining tail length

➤ The single method cast on for left-handed knitters

Just as you can't paint before priming, you also can't start knitting without *casting on* stitches. In this chapter, you'll learn to make the foundation of stitches from which you'll then knit. As you've learned, knitting is joining loops—making enough loops to create fabric. When you cast on, you're making that first row of loops.

This chapter walks you through various cast-on methods, each of which serves a particular purpose in knitting. In addition, a special section helps those who are left-handed make sense of the process.

Once you get the hang of casting on and get your fingers limbered up, move on to the next chapter where you'll learn to work from those stitches to make knitted fabric.

Casting What?

Let's say you want to build a greenhouse in your backyard. Do you start with the roof? The walls? No. You start by laying a solid foundation for your building. The same is true with knitting. Before you can begin knitting, you need a foundation row of stitches from which to knit. You create this row, also called the *selvage*, by casting on stitches.

In this chapter, you'll learn three methods for casting on. Two methods involve casting on by winding yarn around your thumb: the single method and the double method. The third method, called the cable cast-on, actually uses a form of knitting to place the stitches on the needle.

Pointers

If you cast on your stitches too tightly, you'll end with a pinched bottom edge on your finished piece. After you practice knitting a bit, check to see whether the bottom selvage is much tighter and less elastic than the knitted stitches. If so, you'll need to cast on more loosely. To help you make a looser foundation row, cast on stitches using a needle two sizes bigger than the size from which you will be knitting. If the pattern calls for a size 6 needle, for example, use a size 8 needle to cast on.

Needle Talk

Casting on is creating the foundation row of stitches from which you will knit. Casting on is tying a slip knot, attaching the knot to your needle, and adding stitches. The cast-on row is often referred to as *bottom selvage* in instructions.

Many other cast-on methods exist, including such specialties as the multistrand cast-on and the Channel Island cast-on. The three methods you learn in this chapter, however, will serve you well and meet about any knitting need you'll have in the future.

Setting the Stage

You have to cast on before you knit, and to begin casting on, you have to tie a slip knot. This slip knot is how you attach yarn to the needle.

Depending on the method of casting on you choose, you will have either a long or short "tail" of yarn before you tie the slip knot. But we'll get to that soon enough. For now, tie the slip knot about 20" from the end of the yarn.

Here is a tidy three-step method for tying a slip knot.

Loop the yarn around your left index finger.

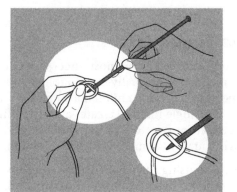

Slip the yarn from your finger and hold the loop between your thumb and index finger.

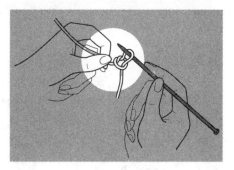

Use the needle, held in your right hand, to draw the loop up and tighten around the needle.

After the knot is on the needle, you can gently tug at both ends of the yarn to lightly tighten the knot. Don't pull too tightly, however. You want the slip knot to be loose enough to move freely on your needle. The loop made from the slip knot is counted as the first stitch on your needle.

45

Pointers

Each of the cast-on methods covered in this chapter gives a bottom selvage that is either elastic or firm. One of these cast-on methods will be ideal depending on your particular project.

The Single Life

The *single method* is the most direct way of casting on. This method is especially easy to follow, making it ideal for beginners. Young children also pick up this cast on well. The single method creates a fairly elastic selvage, so it's perfect for sweaters, jackets, and hats: items for which you want some "give" at the bottom.

Needle Talk

The *tail* is the amount of yarn between the end of the yarn and where something—such as tying a slip knot—occurs. The length of the tail you leave (before tying the slip knot to cast on) differs based on the cast-on method you choose.

To cast on using the single method, begin with the slip knot on your needle. With your right hand, grip the needle that holds the slip knot as you would a wooden spoon. Then follow the steps in these figures:

In your left hand, wrap the yarn that is coming from the skein around your thumb from front to back. Close your left fingers over the yarn in your palm to keep it in place.

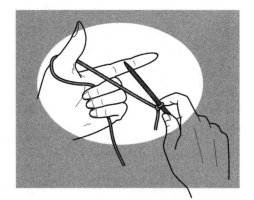

Insert your right hand needle upward through the strand of yarn facing you at the base of your left thumb.

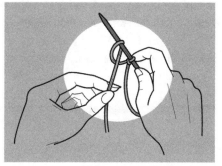

Slip the loop off your thumb onto your needle. Gently pull down on the long strand to tighten the yarn.

Beautiful! You've just cast on your first stitch. You now have two stitches on the needle; the slip knot counts as your first stitch.

Continue this procedure as many times as you want. Try to keep all the stitches uniform by gently pulling down the long strand of yarn after you make each loop. Initially, your stitches will look fairly uneven: Some will be tight and pinched while others will be gaudy and loose. Just keep practicing. It takes time to get the tension even in all the stitches, and you won't get it right the first time out of the gate.

Snarls

Be sure when using both the single method and cable cast-on that you are using the yarn feeding from the skein, not the tail of yarn, to cast on stitches.

Doubles, Anyone?

Now that you feel comfortable with the single method, it's time to learn the *double method*. As you would expect, the double method involves doubles—not thumbs, but two ends of yarn. Your thumb is still a big player here but you will be adding a few fingers to expedite the procedure. Like the single method, the double method creates a fairly elastic selvage, so it's perfect for sweaters, jackets, and hats.

Start with the same slip knot you used for the single method. This time, however, the length of the yarn tail before you tie the slip knot is important; you use the tail to help cast on stitches.

Pointers

The easiest way to determine where to tie the slip knot is to figure 1" of yarn for each stitch you will be casting on. Add an extra 4" so that after you finish casting on, you'll still have a little tail; you'll weave in this tail after you finish knitting. If you want to cast on 20 stitches, start your slip knot 24 inches from the end of the yarn:

20" (20 stitches) + 4" (tail) = 24"

After you have tied a slip knot, follow these steps:

Make a slip knot far enough from the end of the yarn to accommodate 1" per stitch you'll cast on, plus 4".

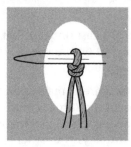

Grasp the shorter end of yarn with your left hand as you did for the single method; wrap it around your thumb and secure it against your palm. Now wrap the yarn from the skein over your right index finger and hold the yarn against your right palm.

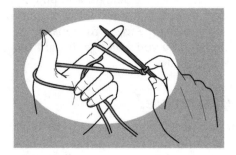

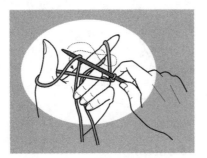

Insert your needle upward at the base of your left thumb, as you did for the single method. Bring the yarn from your index finger over the point of the needle from the back to the front.

With the yarn over the needle, pull the needle through the loop made by your thumb so that the new loop you created is on the needle.

Now gently pull the short end of the yarn to tighten the stitch on the needle. Nice work. You have just completed a double cast-on. You now have two stitches on the needle; the slip knot counts as your first stitch.

Go ahead and practice a few more stitches. If you run out of your yarn tail, just pull out the stitches, tie another slip knot, and start again. Initially, the tension on your stitches is going to vary quite a bit. No big deal. Just keep practicing and soon the stitches will be fairly even.

The Able Cable

The last method of casting on is the *cable cast-on*. This method requires two needles—you'll actually be knitting your stitches onto the needle. The cable cast-on creates a fairly firm selvage, so it works best for items that need a straight, firm edge, such as scarves and afghans.

Pointers

Sometimes a pattern calls for adding more stitches to the edge of a piece—maybe to create a geometrically shaped sweater. In these cases, use the cable cast-on to add the necessary stitches.

To begin, tie a slip knot, leaving about a 4" tail. Then follow the steps in these figures:

Insert the tip of your right-hand needle into the slip knot on your left needle, from front to back, under the left-hand needle.

With your right hand, bring the yarn under and then over the point of the right-hand needle; you now have a loop on the right needle.

Use the right-hand needle to slide the new loop onto the left-hand needle. You now have two loops on the left-hand needle.

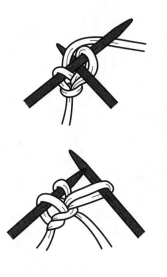

Insert the right-hand needle between the two stitches on your left-hand needle.

Again loop the yarn around the point of the right-hand needle as you did before. Be sure that you insert the right-hand needle between stitch loops on the left-hand needle, rather than through the loops.

Whew! You not only mastered the cable cast-on, but you also just learned the basic process of knitting! You now have two stitches on the needle; the slip knot counts as your first stitch.

Go ahead and keep practicing. If you get bored, rip out the stitches and start again with the slip knot. It's going to feel a little awkward at first, but pretty soon you'll notice you feel comfortable and your stitches look more even.

The Single Method Cast-On with Your Left Hand

The single cast-on is the simplest and most common cast-on method—the one you'll be using most often—but you can also use any of the other cast-on methods in this chapter. Just reverse the instructions so that if the instructions say to do something with your right hand, you do it with your left.

Casting on for left-handed knitters starts with a slip knot—just like it does for right-handed knitters. Because slip knots know no boundaries, what works for the right hand works for the left hand.

To start, make a slip knot, leaving about a 4" tail. You're now ready to cast on a stitch.

With your left hand, grip the needle that holds the slip knot as you would hold a wooden spoon. Then follow these steps:

Grasp the shorter end of yarn with your right hand and wrap it around your thumb from front to back. Then wrap the yarn from the skein over your left index finger and hold both yarn ends with your right palm.

Now insert your needle upward at the base of your right thumb into the loop around your thumb.

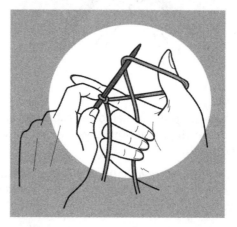

Slip the loop off your thumb onto your needle. Gently pull on the long strand to tighten your stitch.

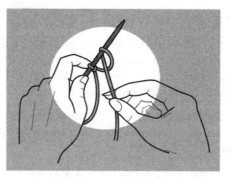

Great! You've just cast on a stitch using the single method. You now have two stitches on the needle; the slip knot counts as your first stitch.

Cast on some more stitches, trying to keep them even. Initially, your stitches are going to vary somewhat: some tight, some loose. Just keep practicing. After a bit, your stitches will even up and you'll feel more comfortable with casting on.

The Least You Need to Know

➤ Casting on means building a foundation of stitches from which you'll knit.

➤ You can cast on one needle, or you can cast on using two needles in a modified knitting style.

➤ It takes practice to get stitches even.

Chapter 6

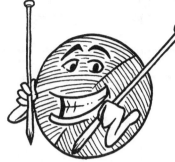

The Big Three: Knitting, Purling, and Binding Off

In This Chapter

➤ Common knit abbreviations

➤ Mastering the noble knit stitch

➤ Playing with purling

➤ Binding off and bringing your work to a graceful close

➤ Left-handed knitting

➤ Garter stitch and stockinette stitch

In Chapter 5, you learned to cast on stitches and get ready to knit.

In this chapter, you're going to learn to knit. Really knit. By the time you finish the chapter, you'll be able to casually let drop at cocktail parties, "Why yes, I do love Glenlivet. And I knit, as well." You'll have something to do with your hands the next rainy Saturday afternoon you spend watching a Joan Crawford moviethon. You'll be a knitter.

Not only that. You'll also know how to purl and bind off stitches. With these three skills, and the cast-on methods you learned in the previous chapter, you'll have everything you need to begin making exquisite pieces.

What are you waiting for? Let's start knitting!

Common Knitting and Purling Abbreviations

The following universal abbreviations will come in handy as you work through the stitches in this chapter. For a full list of knit and crochet abbreviations, see the tearcard at the front of this book.

Abbreviation...	What It Means...
bo	Bind off
k	Knit
p	Purl
rev st st	Reverse stockinette stitch
rs	Right side
st st	Stockinette stitch
ws	Wrong side

Same Stitch, Different Look: Knitting and Purling

As you've learned, knitting is a way of creating fabric using interlocking loops. You've got that.

Knitting and its best buddy purling, which you'll learn about in this chapter, are two complementary ways to join those loops and create more. You knit or purl in rows, using the stitches you cast on the needle.

Here's where things get interesting: Knitting and purling are really the *same* stitch. The only difference lies in whether you pull the end of the loop toward you or move it away from you. A knitted stitch, from the back, looks like a purled stitch; a purled stitch from the back looks like a knitted stitch.

Pointers

Generally speaking, most people find knitting more enjoyable than purling—nothing against purling. Consequently, if you can make the same effect by knitting or purling, pattern designers generally default to having you knit. For example, if you want to make a fabric of all knitted or all purled rows, the instructions will tell you to knit every row rather than purl every row.

This means that if you purl every row, you'll ultimately end up with the same-looking fabric as if you knit every row. This concept might sound confusing, but as you begin watching what your hands are doing, you'll understand how knitting and purling interact to create interesting patterns and effects.

Knitting 101

It's time. You're going to knit. If you plan to knit along with these instructions, cast on about 20 stitches. This is a nice number because it's not so many as to be daunting, but it's enough to see what you're creating.

Getting a Grip

Comfortable knitting begins with properly positioning the yarn and the needles. Follow these instructions:

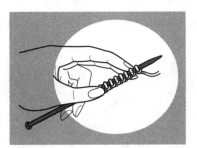

> **Needle Talk**
>
> *Continental knitting* is a different type of knitting from what you are learning in this chapter. In continental knitting, you "catch" the yarn using the needle; you don't use your hand to drape the yarn over the needle. Continental knitting is an incredibly fast and efficient way to knit, but it's often hard for a beginner to learn easily.

With your left hand, grip the needle with the cast-on stitches, lightly holding the first stitch on the needle with your index finger near the point end of the needle.

In your right hand, hold the second needle as you would a pencil.

Place the long end of the yarn over your first finger, under your second, over your third, and under your fourth.

You will want to practice holding your needles with the yarn. When you actually start to work, you will find that you will probably make adjustments as you go, so that everything feels comfortable.

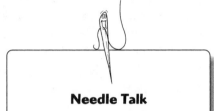

Needle Talk

Knitting is forming rows of interconnecting loops in which the ends of the loops face away from you as you work.

Taking the Plunge

You are now ready to make your first knit stitch. (I hope all this pomp and fanfare won't make knitting—a very easy process—seem anticlimactic.)

To begin, move your hands closer together. Now follow these steps:

Insert the tip of the right-hand needle, front to back, into the first stitch on the left-hand needle—under the left needle.

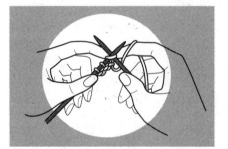

Rest the right-hand needle on top of your left forefinger. The yarn is at the right of your work in your right hand. With your right hand, bring the yarn under and then over the point of the right-hand needle.

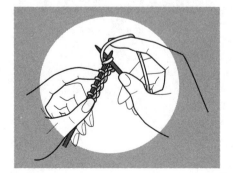

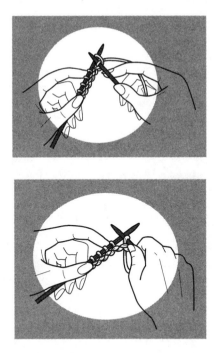

With the help of your left forefinger, slide the point of the right-hand needle back toward you. Using the right-hand needle point, catch the loop made by the yarn over the needle.

Pull the stitch off the left-hand needle. You now have a stitch on the right-hand needle.

Beautiful! You have just knitted your first stitch. The process might seem awkward. In fact, the first stitch on the row always feels a bit awkward—even after you're an experienced knitter. Try another stitch. And another. The process gets easier as you move across the row. In addition, you'll soon find that your right thumb instinctively moves in to steady the new stitch.

Turning Your Work

At some point, you'll run out of stitches on the left needle and you'll have a fresh new row of stitches on your right-hand needle. You are now ready to turn your work so you can knit the second row.

As you turn your work, you will at the same time transfer the needle with the stitches from your right hand to your left hand. You will be looking at the back of the stitches you previously knitted. In this case, because you knit the stitches and the ends of the loops were pointed away from you when you worked the row, they will now be pointed toward you when you turn the stitches; this accounts for the row's bumpy appearance.

Yarn Spinning

Many years ago, when children were routinely taught to knit, a wonderful phrase was taught to make the process easier. Try chanting it; it will help you remember the steps: "In, over, through, and off."

Pointers

Needles are referred to as either right or left, when in actuality they are neither. When the needle is in your right hand it is the "right needle." The same holds true if it should be in your left hand as it would be called your "left needle."

You are now starting over with the empty needle in your right hand and the yarn being held using the technique you learned in the section "Getting a Grip," earlier in this chapter.

Pointers

The only time you don't have to turn your knitting is when you knit in the round—knit in one continuous circle, making either a tubular or circular piece. You'll learn all about knitting in the round in Chapter 11.

When your yarn is in place, repeat the steps for knitting you learned in the section, "Taking the Plunge."

Knitting into a knit stitch on the second row.

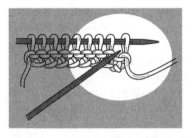

That's it; you're knitting. Can you see how this can become addicting?

Purls of Wisdom

It's time to learn the yin to knitting's yang: the purl stitch. Purling is knitting in reverse: You pull the end of the loop toward you so that the end of the loop faces you. Consequently, the row you're working will have a bumpy texture.

There are two major differences between a knit and a purl stitch. The first is the position of your yarn while you work the stitch. In knitting, the yarn is kept or held to the back of the work. In purling, the yarn is kept or held to the front of the work.

The second difference between the two stitches is where you insert the needle. In knitting, you insert the needle front to back. In purling, you insert it back to front.

To make your first purl stitch use the same yarn and needle positioning you learned in the section, "Getting a Grip." If you plan to purl along with these instructions, cast on about 20 stitches. Bring the yarn forward in front of your right-hand needle. From the right side, insert the tip of the right-hand needle into the front of the first stitch.

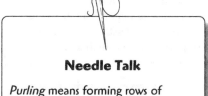

Needle Talk

Purling means forming rows of interconnecting loops in which the ends of the loops face toward you as you work.

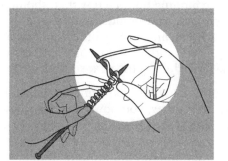

Using your right index finger, wrap the yarn around the right-hand needle counterclockwise.

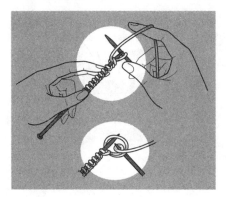

Keeping the new loop on the right-hand needle, slide the point of the right needle backward, down and out. Keep the new loop on your right-hand needle, allowing the original stitch to slide off the left-hand needle.

Needle Talk

Binding off is the process in which you "lock up" all active stitches on the needle so that they can't unravel. You bind off stitches when you're finished with a piece or want to shape an area—such as an armhole in a sweater.

Snarls

Always hold your yarn loosely when binding off. Otherwise, you'll end up with a knitted piece that ends looking pinched and unpleasant. If you find you are an uptight binder-offer, bind off using needles that are one or two sizes larger than the size you used to knit the piece.

From the left side of the stitch, insert the point of your left-hand needle into the first stitch on your right-hand needle.

Wonderful! You have just completed your first purl stitch. Don't worry if you initially feel very awkward working this stitch. Soon it will feel natural.

If you are purling across the row, turn your work when you get to the end of the row, then purl across the next row. Do you notice that this piece worked in all purl stitches looks like the one you worked in all knit stitches?

Bringing It to a Close

Just as you had to work a special row to get ready to knit, you have to work a special row to finish your knitted pieces. This row is made by following a procedure called *binding off*. Binding off actually creates a final row of knitted fabric, so, as you might expect, you bind off differently when you are knitting than when you are purling.

Binding Off in Knitting

If you are binding off on a row that, should you continue working, you would knit instead of purl, use this method. If you are binding off on a row that, should you continue working, you would purl instead of knit, use the procedure in the next section.

To begin binding off in knitting, loosely knit the first 2 stitches in the row; you now have 2 stitches on the right needle. Then follow these steps:

Using the left-hand needle, lift the stitch from the right needle. Bring the stitch up and over the second stitch and off the point of the right-hand needle.

Do you see what you just did? You had 2 stitches on the needle and you looped 1 over the other to end up with only 1 stitch. If you ever made potholders as a kid using those looms with colored nylon loops, you've bound off stitches before, just in a different context.

Here's how to continue binding off across the row:

1. Knit the next stitch on your left needle onto your right-hand needle. You again have 2 stitches on your right-hand needle.

2. Following the preceding illustrations, use your left-hand needle to lift the first stitch on the right-hand needle over the second stitch.

3. Repeat steps 1 and 2 until you have bound off all but 1 stitch.

4. Cut the end of your yarn at least 3" from the needle; pull the yarn end through the last remaining stitch and pull tightly.

You have just secured the last stitch. Your knitted piece now can't unravel.

Binding Off in Purling

Binding off on a row you would otherwise purl is almost exactly like binding off on a row you would otherwise knit.

> Follow the same procedure you learned in the preceding section with one difference: Purl the stitches rather than knit them.

When you have bound off all but one stitch, cut your yarn like you did before, leave a tail, and pull the end of the yarn through your last stitch. That's it!

Pointers

In pattern instructions you will often read, "bind off in pattern." This means that you should bind off in whatever stitch you would use to continue the established pattern. If the row you are working on has both knit and purl stitches, you knit "off" the knits, and purl "off" the purls.

Left-Handed Knitting

Left-handed knitting is like right-handed knitting: easy as pie, after you understand the concept. With the information in this section, along with the casting-on technique you learned in the previous chapter, you'll be knitting like a pro in no time.

The procedures in this section are specifically geared toward those steps that differ from right-handed knitting. Therefore, it's important that you read all the instructions at the beginning of this chapter before you begin.

Your Starting Position

Comfortable knitting begins with properly positioning the yarn and the needles. Follow these instructions:

With your right hand, grip the needle that contains the cast-on stitches, lightly holding the first stitch on the needle with your index finger near the point end of the needle.

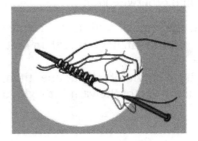

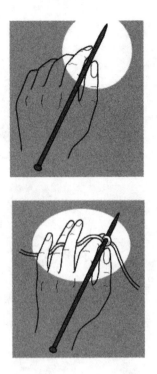

In your left hand, hold the second needle as you would a pencil.

Place the long end of the yarn over your first finger, under your second, over your third, and under your fourth.

How's it feel? This is the position you'll use to begin knitting. It seems a bit strange at first, but soon it'll feel completely natural.

The Knit Stitch

Okay. You're sitting there, holding the needle, the yarn twisted around your fingers at the ready. Now what? You're ready to knit your first stitch! Here's how:

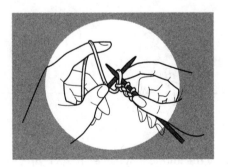

Insert the tip of your left-hand needle, into the first stitch on your right-hand needle, under the right needle.

Rest the right-hand needle on top of your left forefinger. The yarn is at the left of your work in your left hand. Using your left hand, bring the yarn under and then over the point of the left-hand needle.

With the help of your right forefinger, slide the point of the left-hand needle back toward you. Using the left-hand needle point, catch the loop made by the yarn over the needle.

Pull the stitch off the right-hand needle so that it now rests on the left-hand needle. You now have a stitch on the left-hand needle.

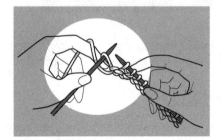

Pointers

When you are ready to bind off, follow the instructions earlier in this chapter for binding off. You need to knit 2 stitches, and then use your left needle to pull the first stitch you knit over the second stitch you knit. Then knit 1 more stitch and pull the first stitch over the second. Continue this way across the row.

Do you feel good? You just produced your first knit stitch! The process might seem awkward. In fact, the first stitch on the row always feels a bit awkward, even after you're an experienced knitter. Try another stitch. And another. The process gets easier as you move across the row. In addition, you'll soon find that your right thumb instinctively moves in to steady the new stitch.

Pointers

If you need clarification on how to do a procedure left-handed, hold a mirror next to the right-handed illustrations so that you can see the image reversed. The reversed image will give you the necessary information you need to work left-handed. If you're lucky enough to have a friend who's a right-handed knitter, sit facing him and mirror his steps.

The Purl Stitch

The purl stitch is almost the same as the knit stitch. Starting as you did with the knit stitch, follow these steps:

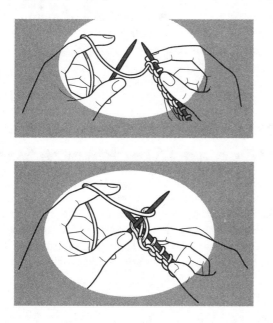

Bring the yarn forward in front of your left-hand needle.

From the left side, insert the left-hand needle point into the back of the first stitch on the right-hand needle. The left needle is in front of the right needle. Using your left index finger, wrap the yarn around the left-hand needle clockwise.

Keeping the new loop on the left-hand needle, slide the point of the left needle backward, down and out. Keep the new loop on your left-hand needle, allowing the original stitch to slide off the right-hand needle.

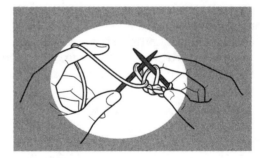

Pointers

When you are ready to bind off, follow the instructions given earlier in this chapter for binding off. You need to purl 2 stitches, and then use your left needle to pull the first stitch you purled over the second stitch you purled. Then purl 1 more stitch and pull the first stitch over the second. Continue this way across the row.

Snarls

Fit to be tied? It can happen. If you are a left-handed knitter and reading directions for right-handed knitting, remember that you *must* substitute the words *right* for *left*, and *left* for *right*. To avoid confusion as you work, use two different colors to highlight the words *right* and *left* in your patterns.

Wonderful! You have just completed your first purl stitch. Don't worry if you initially feel very awkward working this stitch. Soon it will feel natural.

That's it! You're a knitter! And a left-handed knitter, to boot!

The Fabulous Two: Garter Stitch and Stockinette Stitch

At this point, you know how to knit and how to purl. In Chapter 7, you'll learn some impressive ways to combine these stitches on the same row to make patterns in the knitted fabric. Before you get that far, however, let's talk about the two most basic and common of all knitted patterns: garter stitch and stockinette stitch.

Garter Stitch

You create garter stitch by knitting (or purling—but no one does) every row. If you made practice swatches in the knitting and purling sections of this chapter, you have swatches of garter stitch.

Garter stitch is a firm, attractive pattern that is bumpy on both sides of the fabric. If you look closer, however, you'll see that garter stitch actually alternates a smooth row with a bumpy row, but the smooth rows are hard to see. Ridges are the bumpy rows you see on both sides of garter-stitch fabric. Each ridge represents 2 rows of knitting.

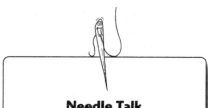

Needle Talk

Garter stitch is a common pattern that is created by knitting every row; it has a fairly bumpy surface. *Stockinette stitch* is another common pattern; it is created by alternating one row of knitting with one row of purling. Stockinette stitch creates a fabric that is smooth on one side and bumpy on the other.

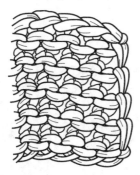

Knitting every row creates garter stitch.

Stockinette Stitch

Stockinette stitch (abbreviated st st) is the stitch that really defines knitting. You're already intimately familiar with this stitch, even if you don't know it. Stockinette stitch is made by alternating one row of knitting with one row of purling. The result is a fabric that is smooth on one side (the *knit side* or *right side*) and bumpy on the other (the *purl side* or *wrong side*). The bumpy side is known as *reverse stockinette stitch*.

Almost everything you own that is knitted is made of stockinette stitch: T-shirts, jersey sheets, many sweaters, stretch pants, sweatshirts… Next time you

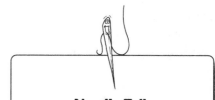

Needle Talk

The *right side* (abbreviated rs) of knitted fabric is the side that will be showing, such as the outside of a sweater. The *wrong side* (abbreviated ws) is the side that faces inward.

put on a T-shirt, take a look at how it's made. You'll notice that the side facing out is smooth, while the inside is comprised of tiny bumps. You're looking at stockinette stitch at work.

Pointers

The knit stitch is slightly thinner and shorter than the purl stitch. This means that the edges of pieces knit in stockinette stitch—where one side is all knit stitches and one side is all purl stitches—curl toward the knit side. Some designers use this natural curling tendency to make sweaters with rolled collars or hats with rolled brims. To anchor stockinette stitch and keep it from curling, you need to edge stockinette stitch pieces either with garter stitch or with a stitch that contains knitting and purling in the same row. Many sweaters feature ribbing to keep edges from rolling.

The knit side of stockinette stitch.

Reverse stockinette stitch.

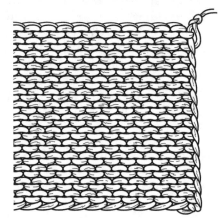

Pointers

When you work in stockinette stitch, you knit the first row and purl the second row. You keep repeating these two rows until you have worked as many rows as you want. If you get confused as to what row you are on, look at your stitches and work them as they appear. If the smooth side is facing you, then you knit. If the bumpy side is facing you, then you purl.

The Least You Need to Know

➤ The knit and purl stitches are really the same stitch, but the method used to create them is different.

➤ Stockinette stitch is created by alternating knit and purl rows. Garter stitch is created by knitting every row.

➤ Binding off is a way to lock up your stitches when you finish a piece.

71

Chapter 7

Special Stitches Using Knitting and Purling

In This Chapter

➤ Common pattern abbreviations

➤ Stitch patterns that combine the knit and purl stitches

➤ Using a cable needle to add a new twist to your knitting

Knitting and purling open the door to all types of special stitches, from simple ribbing at the bottom of a sweater to intricate cabling running up and down an Aran-knit afghan.

In this chapter you'll learn several variations on the knit and purl stitches—how to make interesting patterns by alternating these two stitches.

Then you'll learn one of the most exciting concepts in knitting: using a cable needle to create patterns by knitting stitches out of order.

Common Stitching Abbreviations

The following universal abbreviations will come in handy when you're working with pattern stitches. For a full list of knit and crochet abbreviations, see the tearcard at the front of this book.

Abbreviation...	What It Means...
c2b	Cable 2 back
c4b	Cable 4 back

continues

continued

Abbreviation...	What It Means...
c2f	Cable 2 front
c4f	Cable 4 front
cn	Cable needle
k	Knit
p	Purl
rs	Right side
ws	Wrong side

Simple Patterns That Use the Basic Stitches

In the previous chapter you learned the garter stitch and stockinette stitch. Both these stitches are made by changing how you arrange *rows* of knitting and purling. Now you're going to learn some more stitches that you make by arranging *stitches within a single row*. Most of these patterns will look familiar: They're commonly used in knitted items.

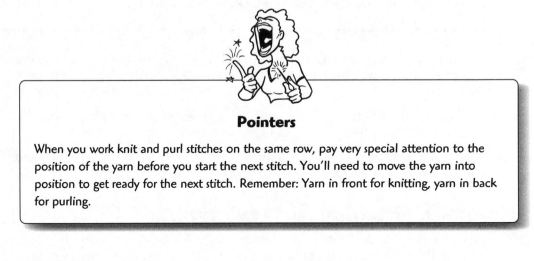

Pointers

When you work knit and purl stitches on the same row, pay very special attention to the position of the yarn before you start the next stitch. You'll need to move the yarn into position to get ready for the next stitch. Remember: Yarn in front for knitting, yarn in back for purling.

Seed Stitch

Seed stitch is a wonderful basic pattern that dresses up plain sweaters or jackets. In addition, because the pattern you create has the same texture on both sides, you can use seed stitch to make beautiful wool scarves or wonderful cotton washcloths.

This pattern, when completed, resembles little seeds scattered across the knit fabric.

Pointers

A *stitch multiple* is the number of stitches necessary to complete a pattern stitch. A pattern of knit 2, purl 2 requires 4 stitches, so it would have a stitch multiple of 4. Often a stitch multiple includes an extra stitch or 2 at the beginning or end of a row of patterned stitches. For example, a stitch multiple of "4 plus 2" means you can start by casting on a number divisible by 4, plus an extra 2 stitches. For this example, you could use 14:

4 (stitch multiple) × 3 (number of times you want to repeat the stitch) + 2 = 14

This means you can work the pattern 3 times, plus have the extra 2 stitches required.

The seed stitch pattern.

Stitch multiple: 2

Row 1 (right side): Knit 1, purl 1. Repeat this pattern across the row.

Row 2 (wrong side): Purl 1, knit 1. Repeat this pattern across the row.

Repeat **Rows 1** and **2** for pattern.

Keep working these two rows as long as you like. Because you are alternating knit and purl stitches, the fabric you create has an even texture all over.

Ribbing

Ribbing is a stitch made by combining knit and purl stitches to form an elastic fabric. This fabric can stretch and then return to its original shape. Ribbing often begins and ends sweater projects, as well as hats, mittens, and socks.

Ribbing uses the same knit 1, purl 1 combination you just used in the seed stitch. Unlike seed stitch, however, you align the knit and purl rows so that you create a vertical texture rather than an overall pattern.

The edges of pieces knit in stockinette stitch roll toward the knit side. This happens because the knit stitches are *slightly* thinner and shorter than the purl stitches, so the piece rolls toward the knit side. To prevent the rolling, pieces knit in stockinette stitch must be edged at the bottom with either garter stitch or a pattern that contains some knitting and purling on every row. This is why you often see sweaters edged in ribbing. The ribbing, being snug and elastic, both keeps the sweater edges from rolling and provides snug, wind-cheating openings.

In this section, you'll learn two variations on the basic rib.

Needle Talk

Barbara Walker, a New Jersey-based writer, spent more than a decade chronicling hundreds of knitting patterns. The sources for her work came from vintage knitting instruction books, her own ideas, and patterns sent in from readers. The result was a trio of knitting pattern encyclopedias. These invaluable volumes went out of print for a bit but have recently been re-released by Schoolhouse Press.

Knit 1, purl 1 ribbing.

Stitch multiple: 2 plus 1

Row 1 (right side): Knit 1. Purl 1, knit 1; repeat these last two stitches across the row.

Row 2 (wrong side): Purl 1. Knit 1, purl 1; Repeat these last two stitches across the row.

Repeat **Rows 1** and **2** for pattern.

Keep working these two rows as long as you like. The fabric you create looks a lot like the bottom of your favorite sweater. When you grow weary of ribbing, try alternating knit and purl rows to get an idea of how a sweater is created.

Pointers

When working in rib, you work your stitches as they appear. In other words, if you're about to work into a smooth stitch in which the loop end is facing away from you, you knit this stitch. If you are about to work into a bumpy stitch in which the loop end faces toward you, you purl this stitch. In ribbing, the knit stitches are prominent and the purl stitches recede between the knit stitches.

The elasticity of ribbing is determined by how far apart you place the knit and purl stitches. The farther apart, the less "give" in the ribbing. You're now going to try a ribbing with a little less give: knit 2, purl 2 ribbing. This creates ribs that are—as you might expect—twice as wide as knit 1, purl 1 ribbing.

Knit 2, purl 2 ribbing.

Stitch multiple: 4 plus 2

Row 1 (right side): Knit 2. Purl 2, knit 2; repeat these last 4 stitches across the row.

Row 2 (wrong side): Purl 2. Knit 2, purl 2; Repeat these last 4 stitches across the row.

Repeat **Rows 1** and **2** for pattern.

Keep working these 2 rows as long as you like. The ribs are thicker than in the knit 1, purl 1 ribbing, but the fabric you create is still very elastic.

77

Checkers, Anyone?

In ribbing, you work your patterns vertically. When you make the checkerboard pattern, however, you form blocks or squares rather than vertical lines. The checkerboard pattern makes a visually interesting pattern that looks the same on the front and back of the fabric. This pattern is great for dishcloths, washcloths, afghans, and scarves. In fact, if you want to see a variation of this pattern in action, try the checkerboard scarf pattern in Chapter 8.

You begin working this pattern the same way you work Knit 1, purl 2 ribbing. After several rows, however, you alternate the placement of the pattern.

The versatile checkerboard pattern.

Stitch multiple: 4 plus 2

Row 1: (right side) Knit 2. Purl 2, knit 2; repeat these last 4 stitches across the row.

Row 2: (wrong side) Purl 2. Knit 2, purl 2; repeat these last 4 stitches across the row.

Row 3: Repeat **Row 1**.

Row 4: Repeat **Row 1**.

Row 5: Repeat **Row 2**.

Row 6: Repeat **Row 1**.

Repeat **Rows 1–6** for pattern.

Keep repeating these 6 rows until you grow tired of working the checkerboard pattern.

Notice how this pattern lies flat, whereas in ribbing the knit and purl columns are much more distinct. This is much of the fun in trying new stitches—depending on how you arrange the knit and purl stitches, you can come up with many different and compelling effects.

Cable Knitting

Cable knitting has a reputation for being complex and advanced. While some very intricate patterns are a challenge even for experienced knitters, the basic cable stitch is easy and rewarding. The pattern uses a combination of knit and purl stitches, which are then physically rearranged ("crossed over") on the fabric. The process you'll learn here is the basis of many specialized types of knitting, including the intricate Aran sweaters from Ireland.

To produce a cable, you'll need one piece of specialized equipment: a cable needle. (If you've forgotten what this is, flip back to Chapter 4.) If you don't have a cable needle, you can use either a double-pointed needle or a crochet hook, but the process will be a bit more awkward.

While the strategy you're going to learn here can be applied to knitting any stitches out of order and creating eye-popping effects of texture, we'll just be making a very simple cable. This type of cable is worked in stockinette stitch, with the knitted stitches on the right side of the fabric being cabled. For the cables to stand out, plan on at least 2 purl stitches on either side of your cable panel.

> ### Needle Talk
>
> *Cables* are specialized knitting patterns created by physically moving stitches and knitting them out of their original order. In the cable's simplest form, the first half of a group of stitches is placed on "hold" while the second half is worked. The stitches on hold are then worked, creating a spiral effect. The *cable panel* is the stockinette stitch column on which the cable is worked.

Cable 4 Back (c4b)

The first of the two basic cables is a cable 4 back (c4b). This stitch makes a cable that twists to the right. In the next section you'll learn to make a cable 4 front (c4f), which produces a cable that twists to the left.

The following instructions might seem cumbersome. Don't get discouraged reading them: It takes longer to explain cables then it does to make them.

Stitch multiple: 6 plus 2

Row 1 (right side): Purl 2. Knit 4, purl 2; repeat the last 6 stitches across the row. (The 4 stitches you just knit are the cable panel.)

Row 2 (wrong side): Knit 2. Purl 4, knit 2; repeat the last 6 stitches across the row.

Row 3: Repeat **Row 1**.

Row 4: Repeat **Row 2**.

Row 5: Purl 2. Now complete these steps that follow to make your first cable. This is called a cable 4 back, abbreviated c4b:

Slip the next 2 stitches onto a cable needle and hold the cable needle in the back of your work.

Knit the next 2 stitches from the left-hand needle.

Now knit the 2 stitches from your cable needle.

To finish Row 5, purl 2. Continue across the row, making the cable and purling 2, to the end of the row.

Row 6: Repeat **Row 2.**

Very easy, isn't it? And can you see how using a cable needle can enable you to move stitches all over your knitted fabric, cabling up and down and across? This technique is a great one for you to casually pull out in the company of people you want to impress: Your mastery of not two but three needles will have everyone impressed with your knitting prowess.

Cable 4 Front (c4f)

The cable 4 front (c4f) stitch is almost identical to the cable 4 back, with two exceptions: You hold the stitches on the cable needle in front of your work, and the stitch produces a pattern that twists to the left.

Stitch multiple: 6 plus 2

Row 1 (right side): Purl 2. Knit 4, purl 2; repeat the last 6 stitches across the row. (The 4 stitches you knit are the cable panel.)

Row 2 (wrong side): Knit 2. Purl 4, knit 2; repeat these last 6 stitches across the row.

Row 3: Repeat **Row 1**.

Row 4: Repeat **Row 2**.

Row 5: Purl 2. Now complete the following steps to make the cable. This is called a cable 4 front, abbreviated c4f:

Yarn Spinning

One of the most enduring and romantic notions regarding knitting lore is, apparently, also untrue. Legend claims that intricate Aran sweaters were knit using family patterns that could help identify the washed-up bodies of drowned fisherman. In reality, historians now believe that the Aran sweater as we know it was probably a 20th-century commercial venture, and fisherman most likely wore ganseys, a more movement-friendly sweater.

Slip the next 2 stitches onto a cable needle and hold the cable needle in the front of your work.

Knit the next 2 stitches from the left-hand needle.

Now knit the 2 stitches
from the cable needle.

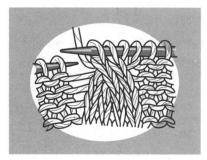

To finish Row 5, purl 2. Continue across the row, making the cable and purling 2, to the end of the row.

Row 6: Repeat **Row 2**.

Pointers

When working cables, you have to allow enough rows between your cable twist so that you can work the twist and keep the cable in a spiral. The greater the number of stitches in the cable panel, the more rows you need between cable twists. Pattern instructions will tell you how often to work the twist.

Have fun working your cables. When you finish working cable patterns, bind off the stitches on the right side of the fabric.

The Least You Need to Know

➤ You can make numerous stitch patterns by strategically placing knit and purl stitches on a row.

➤ How stitches are placed determines their final appearance: whether flat like the checkerboard pattern or alternately raised and recessed like ribbing.

➤ Ribbing generally edges the bottom, neck, and cuffs of sweaters because it provides an elastic edge and makes the sweater cozier.

➤ You make cables by using a cable needle to change the order in which you knit stitches.

Whip Up a Neck-Loving Scarf

It's inevitable. Every new knitter has to make a scarf. Think about it: They're rectangular, or, for new knitters, relatively square—meaning no shaping. They're useful. Gauge is relatively unimportant. They make great gifts for significant others who are proud of your newfound skills. They let you play with saucy novelty yarns without worrying about shaping a garment.

This scarf is a bit special because you won't be creating the classic garter stitch scarf most knitters begin with. Instead, you'll make a fun checkerboard-patterned scarf that hides mistakes well but looks like it came from a more advanced knitter.

So, stop putting it off and get started on your scarf!

Pointers

If you've forgotten, garter stitch is created when you knit every row of a flat piece of knitting.

What Do I Need?

These scarves are fabulous because you can make an infinite number of variations by changing the yarn, needle size, or—in some cases—the number of stitches that you cast on. You'll learn more about the variations at the end of this chapter.

Snarls

After you have a little more experience knitting, you might want to try this pattern in a fun mohair. Because the long hairs of mohair don't enable you to see stitches clearly—something crucial for new knitters—you'll save yourself a lot of frustration by steering clear of mohair your first time out.

To make a basic scarf about 6 inches wide by about 60 inches long, you'll need only three supplies:

➤ About 7 or 8 ounces (250 to 300 yards) of bulky yarn. Choose any yarn you like. I made one sample using two skeins of Reynolds Lopi. Another was made in Artisan, a yarn made by Classic Elite. Another was made in a multicolored worsted merino wool from Morehouse Farms in Red Hook, New York. Choose any yarn that is attractive, that feels nice, and that will knit up to somewhere around 4 stitches to the inch.

➤ Straight, single-pointed needles in size 8, 9, or 10. The smaller the needle, the narrower the scarf will be, but any of these sizes is fine.

➤ A yarn needle for weaving in the ends at the beginning and end of the project.

Pointers

Many knitters find that yarn slips less on wood needles than on aluminum ones. If you're buying new needles especially for this project, consider buying wood.

How Do I Make It?

This scarf uses a checkerboard design, which is also called a basketweave design. You make even squares of stockinette stitch and reverse stockinette stitch. The process is simple, but the results are impressive.

You can make different sizes of checkerboards. Here is a two-stitch-wide design; your scarf has a four-stitch-wide design.

Start by casting on 24 stitches. You can actually cast on a greater or lesser number of stitches, so long as that number is divisible by 8. For this first outing, however, go ahead and cast on 24 stitches; this will give you a scarf that is approximately 6 inches wide.

Rows 1 through 4: Follow this pattern across the entire row: Knit 4, purl 4. Because you have cast on 24 stitches, you'll actually do the following:

knit 4, purl 4, knit 4, purl 4, knit 4, purl 4

Rows 5 through 8: Follow this pattern across the entire row: Purl 4, knit 4. Because you have cast on 24 stitches, you'll actually do the following:

purl 4, knit 4, purl 4, knit 4, purl 4, knit 4

Snarls

If your counting gets off slightly, you might forget to change patterns every 4 rows and end up with a couple checks that are slightly taller than the other checks. Don't sweat it. This pattern is very forgiving; no one but you will know about the difference in check height.

You'll start to see a checkerboard pattern emerging on the scarf. Because you're working with a thick yarn, that pattern emerges fairly quickly.

At some point you will need to add on a new skein of yarn. When you see you're running low, finish the current row using the first skein. Then begin knitting the next row with the second skein. A couple stitches into the row, you can loosely tie (don't knot!) the two ends together. When you finish the project, you'll use a yarn needle to weave the ends into the finished scarf.

Next-to-last row: When the scarf is as long as you want it, finish up the next full block of checks (knit either a Row 4 or a Row 8).

Final Row: Bind off the 24 stitches on the needle.

Pointers

To help you keep track of count, you can tick rows on a sheet of paper. When you get to 4 ticks, you know it's time to change the pattern: from beginning the row with knit 4 to beginning with purl 4, or vice versa.

To finish: Use a yarn needle to work the yarn ends into the scarf so that they don't show.

Pointers

Here's how the pattern would look abbreviated. Soon you'll be able to read patterns like this:

co 24. Rows 1–4: (k4, p4) to end. Rows 5–8: (p4, k4) to end. Work these 8 rows to desired length. End with Row 4 or Row 8. Bind off.

Variations on a Theme

Want to get adventuresome? Try these modifications:

➤ If you're not feeling up to knitting and purling, just knit every row. You'll create a beautiful, homey, nubby scarf of all garter stitch. Rustic wool looks great in garter stitch.

➤ If you want to make this scarf more luxurious, try working it in a chenille yarn. Harlequin chenille is a beautiful, multicolored yarn that works up wonderfully in this pattern on a size 8 needle. You'll definitely want to use wooden needles if you use a chenille yarn: Chenille slides all over metal needles like a car on a rainy highway.

➤ Knit with two strands of yarn together to create a beautiful blended color. You might, for example, find two gorgeous sport weight yarns—one in purple, one in blue—and combine them for a knockout glamorous result.

Pointers

If terms such as "sport weight" and "chunky" have you feeling faint, turn to Chapter 2 for a quick refresher course on available yarn thicknesses.

➤ For a little added pizzazz, turn to Chapter 18 and follow the directions for adding fringe.

➤ Try knitting with a variegated yarn to create color blasts without worrying yourself with changing colors.

➤ After you make the scarf in bulky yarn, try it with smaller needles (say, size 5 or 6) and a worsted-weight yarn. Cast on more stitches, in multiples of 8. For example, you might cast on 40 stitches instead of 24. The scarf worked in a smaller yarn on smaller needles has a greater number of checks, giving it a different-looking texture.

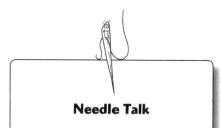

Needle Talk

Variegated yarn is yarn dyed with many varying colors—blending from, say, yellow to green to blue.

The Least You Need to Know

➤ You don't have to be a knitting expert to make a professional-looking, wearable scarf.

➤ With this basic pattern you have a world of knitting opportunities open to you simply by changing the yarn, the needle size, or the number of stitches you cast on.

➤ You can track the rows you're on by ticking the row count on a piece of paper.

Chapter 9

What Goes Up Must Come Down: Increasing and Decreasing

In This Chapter

➤ Understanding common increase and decrease abbreviations

➤ Adding stitches...intentionally

➤ Discreetly decreasing stitches

➤ Using increase and decrease stitches decoratively

Knitting and purling—and all the variations you learned for them—can keep you on the straight and narrow for as far as you want to go. By knowing these two stitches, you can create beautiful scarves, ornamental afghans, and even simple sweaters. But, as you might have guessed, knitting doesn't limit you to making only squares and rectangles. Instead, you can make your knitted pieces nearly any form you want by shaping them through increasing and decreasing stitches.

In this chapter you'll learn the basic procedures for increasing and decreasing stitches. In addition, however, you'll also learn how to use increasing and decreasing stitches to create interesting patterns in your knitting.

Common Increase/Decrease Abbreviations

The following abbreviations are commonly used to indicate increasing and decreasing stitches. For a full list of knit and crochet abbreviations, see the tearcard at the front of this book.

Abbreviation...	What It Means...
dec	Decrease
inc	Increase
k2Tog	Knit 2 together
m1	Make 1
psso	Pass slipped stitch over
sl	Slip
ssk	Slip Slip Knit
yo	Yarn over

The following sections explain what all this chicken scratch means.

When Too Much Isn't Enough: Increasing

You'll often find yourself increasing the number of stitches: As you shape a sleeve from the wrist up, for example, or as you make the thumb gusset on a mitten. This section covers three common types of increases: yarn over, bar increases, and make 1.

Yarn Over (yo)

Yarn over is the simplest way to increase, and it creates a lacy "hole" in the fabric. Obviously, you only want to use a yarn-over increase if you *want* a lacy hole in the fabric. The knitted dishcloth in Chapter 10 is an excellent example of using yarn over to increase the number of stitches on your needle and create a decorative edge at the same time.

To yarn over when knitting, get ready to knit the next stitch, but don't insert the right-hand needle into the loop on the left-hand needle. Wrap the yarn over the needle. The needle now has an extra loop on it.

Yarn-over increases are accomplished by wrapping the yarn over the needle, creating an extra stitch and a lacy hole.

Pointers

The fastest buttonhole you can make for a baby sweater is by making a yarn over and then knitting the next 2 stitches together (k2Tog, which you'll learn about later in this chapter). Knitting with size 6 or so needles and worsted weight yarn, this buttonhole accommodates about a ¹/₂-inch button.

Continue knitting the row as usual. On the next row, when you knit into the extra loop, the hole will appear.

To make a yarn over by purling, wrap the yarn from the front of the needle to the back, under the needle, and back to the front. Then continue purling.

Bar Increase

A bar increase is called such because you literally create a "bar" of yarn where you increase. The bar increase is fairly unnoticeable and creates no decorative hole, making it perfect for increasing when you want to discreetly add stitches without calling attention to the increases.

Pointers

The bar increase is the default increase. In other words, if a pattern indicates that you should increase stitches, but it doesn't indicate which stitch to use, you can safely use the bar increase.

Here's how to make a bar increase when knitting:

1. Prepare to knit a stitch. Insert the right-hand needle into the *front* of the first loop on the left-hand needle, pull the new stitch through the old stitch, but don't yet slide the stitch off the left-hand needle.

   If you're knitting left-handed, reverse the left and right needle designations.

Beginning a bar increase by knitting into the front of a stitch.

2. Now insert the point of the right-hand needle into the *back* of the first stitch on the left-hand needle and complete another knit stitch.

Knitting into the back of the same stitch.

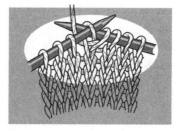

3. Now slide the stitch off the left-hand needle. You'll have 2 stitches on the right-hand needle for the 1 stitch you had on the left-hand needle.

If you need to increase a stitch while purling a row, simply purl into the back and front of the stitch.

Make 1 (m1)

Make 1 is the trickiest of the increase stitches, but also the most versatile. This stitch creates a nearly invisible increase if done one way, or a decorative hole if done another way. The idea behind m1 is that you are *making* a stitch from the knitted fabric where one didn't exist. Get it?

Here's all you need to do:

1. Find the horizontal line of yarn between the stitch on the left needle and the stitch on the right.

Finding the horizontal line between the stitches on the right-hand and left-hand needles.

2. Insert the tip of the right-hand needle into this line; then pull the line onto the left-hand needle, making an extra stitch on that needle.

Pulling the horizontal line onto the left needle.

3. If you want to create a decorative hole, knit into the *front* of this new stitch and slide the stitch off the left-hand needle onto the right-hand needle.

   If you want no hole, knit into the *back* of this new stitch and slide the stitch off the left-hand needle onto the right-hand needle.

Completing the increase.

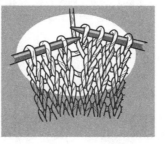

Losing the Girth: Decreasing

So what if you need to get rid of stitches rather than add them? This section covers three common types of decreases: knit two together (k2Tog); slip slip knit (ssk); and slip, knit, pass slipped stitch over (sl, k, psso).

Knit Two Together (k2Tog)

Knit 2 together is the simplest and most common way to decrease stitches. As the name implies, you are knitting two stitches together. This stitch causes a decrease that leans to the right.

Pointers

Knit 2 together is the default decrease. In other words, if a pattern indicates that you should decrease stitches, but it doesn't indicate which stitch to use, you can safely use knit 2 together.

Knitting 2 stitches together.

To decrease this way while purling, purl 2 stitches together.

Purling 2 stitches together.

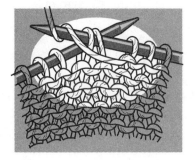

Slip Slip Knit (ssk)

Slip slip knit is exactly what it sounds like. You slip, you slip, and then you knit. The trick involves what you slip and how you knit. This stitch causes a decrease that leans to the left. Here's how you do it:

1. Insert the right-hand needle into the first loop on the left-hand needle, as if you were going to knit; slip the stitch onto the right-hand needle. Do the same thing with the next stitch on the needle. You now have two stitches that haven't been knitted on the right-hand needle.

Slipping a stitch.

2. Now insert the left-hand needle through both loops on the right-hand needle.

3. Bring the yarn around and knit the stitch, keeping the new stitch on the right-hand needle.

Knitting the 2 slipped stitches from the right-hand needle.

Slip, Knit, Pass Slipped Stitch Over (sl, k, psso)

As with slip slip knit, this decrease makes a stitch that slants to the left. Here's how you do it:

1. Insert the right-hand needle into the first loop on the left-hand needle, as if you were going to knit; slip the stitch onto the right-hand needle.

Slipping a stitch.

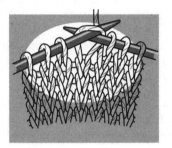

2. Knit the next stitch.

3. Now insert the left-hand needle into slipped stitch.

Inserting the needle into the slipped stitch.

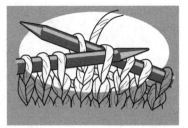

4. Using the needle, bring the slipped stitch over the knitted stitch.

Passing the slipped stitch over the knitted stitch.

5. Pull the slipped stitch off the right-hand needle, and then release the stitch.

When Increasing and Decreasing Don't Do Either

Have you tried some of the increase and decrease procedures throughout this chapter? You might have noticed, then, that several of the stitches not only add or subtract stitches on the needle, but they also slightly change the look of the knitted fabric. Suppose, then, that on a row you increase and decrease the same number of stitches but place those increases and decreases strategically to create a specific pattern. Do you know what you'd get? Lace.

Look at this illustration. This simple gull-wing lace is a repeat of 7 stitches. To create the pattern, the knitter increased and decreased the same number of stitches in each row by using techniques you learned in this chapter: yarn over (yo), knit 2 together (k2Tog), and slip slip knit (ssk).

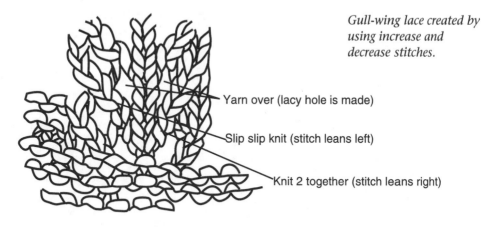

Gull-wing lace created by using increase and decrease stitches.

Yarn over (lacy hole is made)

Slip slip knit (stitch leans left)

Knit 2 together (stitch leans right)

Pointers

To try the gull-wing pattern yourself, cast on any number of stitches that is divisible by 7 (such as 14, 21, or 28). The pattern is 7 stitches long, and you repeat this pattern across the row. **First row:** k1, k2Tog, yo, k1, yo, ssk, k1. **Second Row:** Purl. **Third Row:** k2Tog, yo, k3, yo, ssk. **Fourth Row:** Purl.

The Least You Need to Know

➤ With a few simple techniques, you can shape your knitting using increasing and decreasing stitches.

➤ Different increasing and decreasing stitches are appropriate for different tasks.

➤ You can strategically use increasing and decreasing stitches to create a pattern within knitted fabric rather than to shape the fabric.

Chapter 10

Make a Knitted Cotton Dishcloth

In This Chapter

➤ The supplies you'll need to get started

➤ How to make a smashing dishcloth

➤ Additional variations and ideas with your basic pattern

Did you read the title of this chapter and snort, "Dishcloths? Who wants to make dishcloths?" Not so fast. These cloths are addicting. Pretty soon you'll find yourself scoping Sunday sale papers, looking for specials on cotton yarn. You'll find you stop using the dishwasher so that you can wear out cloths quicker, necessitating the production of more. You'll begin stringing together the cloths to make attractive ensembles to wear Saturday nights on the town.

The dishcloth you're about to make has a host of advantages: It allows you to finish a project quickly; it lets you practice basic knitting as well as increasing and decreasing; it's infinitely usable and practical; it makes a great gift; and, if the yarn is bought on sale, it costs about 50 cents to produce. In addition, its construction is interesting: Rather than knitting from top to bottom in a square, you knit from one corner to the other. Are you intrigued? Let's go!

What Do I Need?

You'll need very little to make these dishcloths. I give you needle suggestions, but *needle size and gauge aren't tremendously important*. If a dishcloth is a little bigger or smaller than you planned, big deal.

To make a cloth that's about 7 inches square, you'll need these supplies:

➤ About $1^1/_4$ ounces (60 yards) of bulky cotton yarn. Two popular brands of bulky cotton are Sugar'n Cream and Bernat Handicrafter. Both of these brands go on sale periodically at craft superstores such as Michael's and Hobby Lobby. One solid-colored $2^1/_2$ skein of Sugar'n Cream provides enough yarn for two dishcloths.

Pointers

Most yarns in solid colors come in slightly larger skeins than ombre or variegated yarn. For example, solid-color Sugar 'n Cream cotton is sold in 2¹/₂-ounce skeins, but variegated Sugar'n Cream is sold in 2-ounce skeins.

➤ Straight, single-pointed needles in size 6, 7, 8, 9, or 10. Being a particularly vigorous dish washer, I prefer size 6 needles because the resulting dishcloths are fairly firm and tight and wear longer, but any size in this range will do. Why not split the difference and use a size 8 needle? If you're buying new needles for this project, buy wood; cotton can be a tiny bit slick, and it slides less on wooden needles than on aluminum ones.

➤ A yarn needle for weaving in the ends at the beginning and end of the project.

How Do I Make It?

Start by casting on 4 stitches. (How in the world will you make a large dishcloth with only 4 stitches? Stick with me; it works.)

Row 1: Knit across. This row might be a little tricky to knit because the stitches feel very big and very loose. Don't worry about it.

Row 2: Knit 2 stitches. In the next stitch, knit into the front and then the back of the stitch (1 bar increase made). Knit the last stitch on the row.

Row 3: Knit 2 stitches. Yarn over (1 bar increase made). Knit to the end of the row.

Pointers

If you forget how to do a yarn over (also called a "Yo!"), turn to Chapter 9.

Repeat **Row 3** until you have 46 stitches on the needle. You have a triangle at this point, and the long edge of the triangle is on your needle.

Next row: Knit 1 stitch, knit together the next 2 stitches (1 decrease made), yarn over (1 increase made), knit 2 stitches together (1 decrease made), knit to the end of the row.

Repeat this last row until 5 stitches remain on the needle.

Next row: Knit 2 stitches, knit the next 2 stitches together (1 decrease made), knit the last stitch.

Last row: Bind off the 4 stitches on the needle.

To finish: Use a yarn needle to work the yarn ends into the dishcloth so that they don't show.

Weaving in the ends is the last step; now your dishcloth is finished!

Pointers

Here's how the pattern would look abbreviated. Soon you'll be able to read patterns like this:

co 4. k 1 row. In next row, k2, inc in next st, k1. In next row, k2, yo, k to end of row; repeat this row until 46 sts are on needle. Next row, k1, k2Tog, yo, k2Tog, k to end of row. Repeat this row until 5 stitches remain. k2, k2Tog, k1. Bind off 4 sts.

Variations on a Theme

Want to get adventuresome? Try some of these variations:

➤ Increase the number of stitches—say to about 55—and create a fabulous facecloth. If you're really ambitious, turn to Chapter 17 and make a crochet chain of about 8 stitches; fold the chain in half and sew it on a corner of the facecloth to make a hanging loop.

➤ Knit up batches of these dishcloths; they make great TV-watching fare once you get down the concept. Combine three or more brightly colored dishcloths in a basket with a bottle of hand lotion and some kitchen soap. Voila! You have an instant, thoughtful, and inexpensive housewarming gift.

➤ Try new pattern stitches by making cotton swatches that can then be used as dishcloths.

Pointers

Hungry to try more? Check out **http://www.keyway.net/crafts/Facecloth.htm** on the Web. You'll find patterns for several dozen cloths—many with pictures showing how the finished cloth will look—all using the same inexpensive cotton yarn.

The Least You Need to Know

➤ You can knit a stunning, usable piece with your limited knitting experience!

➤ Dishcloths and facecloths make savvy, usable homemade gifts.

➤ You can play with different patterns to create unique dishcloths without investing lots of time or money.

Part 3

Taking the Next Step: More Complex Knitting

Are you hungry for more knitting adventure? This section takes you past straight, one-color stitching and into some more advanced topics: adding color, knitting seamless tubes, and reading those Arabic-looking knitting patterns. To try your new skills, knit up a fun roll-brim hat; all the instructions are in this section.

In addition, everyone makes mistakes and most common mistakes are easily fixable. In this section, you'll also learn what to do when you make one: when to salvage your work and when to rip it out.

Chapter 11

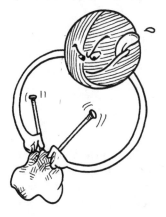

Knitting in the Round

In This Chapter

➤ Common in-the-round abbreviations

➤ The advantages of knitting in the round

➤ Joining with a circular needle

➤ Using double-pointed needles

At times, working back and forth, knitting flat pieces of fabric, isn't going to meet all your needs. For example, although you *can* knit a pair of socks back and forth using two needles, and then sew up a back seam, working the socks in a seamless tube will ultimately be easier for you and more comfortable for the wearer.

In this chapter, you'll learn the benefits of knitting in the round. You'll also learn how to use the correct tools—double-pointed needles and circular needles—to do so.

By the end of this chapter, you might be itching to try some in-the-round knitting of your own. If so, turn to Chapter 13 and try your hand at a simple but attractive roll-brim hat.

Common In-the-Round Abbreviations

The following universal abbreviations will come in handy when you're working in the round. For a full list of knit and crochet abbreviations, see the tearcard at the front of this book.

Abbreviation...	What It Means...
dpn	Double-pointed needle
pm	Place marker
rnd	Round

Why Go 'Round and 'Round?

Knitting in the round has many advantages you don't get with flat knitting. So many, in fact, that some knitters all but refuse to work pieces flat. Much of the popularity of circular-needle knitting was started by knitting legend Elizabeth Zimmermann, who encouraged knitters to work flat only when it couldn't be avoided—and then to work flat on circular needles.

While I won't go so far as to ban you from using straight needles, knitting in the round does have these benefits:

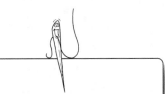

Needle Talk

Elizabeth Zimmermann, a self-proclaimed "opinionated knitter," has done much to increase knitting's popularity over the past three decades. Her knitting camps, video workshops, *Woolgathering* newsletter, and numerous books continue to teach beginning and experienced knitters new techniques and a love for the craft. Ms. Zimmermann retired in the late 1980s and her daughter *Meg Swansen* continues to run the family knitting business.

➤ **You get to use the knit stitch more.** Most pieces are made of stockinette stitch (knit one row, purl one row), or some variation, and most knitters eventually find that they enjoy making the knit stitch better than they enjoy making the purl stitch. Unfortunately, knitting flat stockinette stitch pieces requires half your stitches to be purled. When you knit in the round, however, you are in essence knitting one long, continuous row. Consequently, you never need to purl unless you're making a pattern in the knitted fabric.

➤ **Finishing on some pieces is often minimal.** Let's say you're making a sweater. If you knit the pieces flat, you'll eventually need to sew up at least six seams: two arm seams, two joining seams of arms and body, and the left and right body seams. Now look at a sweater knit in the round. You need to sew up two tiny seams only; the rest of your time is spent knitting.

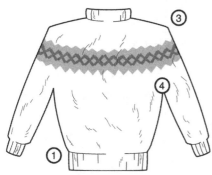

1. Body is knit in a tube.

2. Sleeves are knit in tubes.

3. Sleeves and body are joined on one circular needle and yoke is knit.

4. Small seams at underarms joining body and sleeves are sewn.

Knitting in the round often lets you spend more time knitting than sewing.

➤ **You can see how a piece will fit.** Unlike straight needles, circular needles are flexible. As you're working, you can step into a pullover sweater knit in the round and make sure it fits. Working pieces flat, you have to do a bit more guessing about size.

➤ **Some pieces are simply better constructed when made in seamless tubes.** Socks, mittens, and the necks on turtlenecks are all more ideally made in a tube without a seam to either irritate the wearer or break the flow of the knitted fabric.

So now that you see how circular knitting might be beneficial, let's do some.

Knitting on a Circular Needle

For new knitters, working on a circular needle is a much easier way to knit in the round than working with a set of four or five double-pointed needles. You only have one needle to navigate, and you never have to worry about stitches looking consistent, as you sometimes must when knitting on double-pointed needles.

Pointers

When knitting on a circular needle, you must be conscientious of needle length. When you knit on straight needles, you can use the part of the needle you need (such as using 14" needles to knit a scarf 7" wide). When knitting tubes on circular needles, the needle must be the same size or slightly smaller than the item you're knitting. If it's much smaller, you could have trouble keeping stitches on the needle. If it's much larger, you'll stretch your fabric. When knitting on circular needles, you may need to change to needles of different lengths—or even double-pointed needles—as you increase or decrease.

To knit on a circular needle, follow these steps:

1. Cast on the number of stitches required by the pattern. Slide a stitch marker onto the left-hand end of the needle. This marker indicates the start of every new row.

2. Lay the circular needle on a flat surface and make sure that the cast-on stitches are all facing inward—toward the middle of the circle. Check very carefully to make sure that the cast-on row is straight and that none of the stitches are twisted around the needle.

    The tail of the yarn should be on the left side, and the yarn coming from the skein should be on the right. If you're knitting left-handed, reverse these instructions.

Make sure that the stitches aren't twisted before you begin knitting.

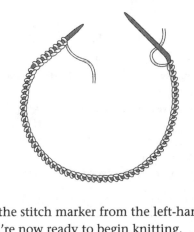

3. Carefully pick up the needle. Slip the stitch marker from the left-hand side of the needle to the right-hand side. You're now ready to begin knitting.

4. Knit the first stitch from the left-hand side of the needle to the right-hand side. You've now joined the circle. Knit around the circle.

Beginning to knit in the round.

5. When you finish the first round and come to the stitch marker, slide it from the left to the right tip and keep knitting.

That's it! You're knitting in the round.

You can also use circular needles to knit flat pieces. Often when you're knitting extremely large pieces, such as afghans, you'll need the extra needle real-estate that a 29" circular needle can provide. To knit flat pieces on a circular needle, pretend that the two ends of the circular needle are two single-pointed straight needles. Turn your work as you normally would, and work from one side of the needle to the other.

Knitting on Double-Pointed Needles

You may never need to knit on double-pointed needles. Circular needles now come in sizes so small you can knit socks on them. For some knitters, however, these needles can be hard to use—your hands may feel like they're all over each other in the middle of a tiny tube of fabric. You also need to learn to use double-pointed needles because you will need to use them if you are beginning or ending a circle of fabric. For example, if you're knitting a cap, you'll need to use double-pointed needles for the very top where the tube of fabric closes over the top of your head.

Although knitting on double-pointed needles isn't harrowing, it can be a challenge for new knitters. Be patient with yourself as you add this new skill to your knitting repertoire.

Here's how to use double-pointed needles:

1. Cast on all the stitches onto one needle. If you are making a piece small enough so that all the stitches fit onto one double-pointed needle, go ahead and use one. Otherwise, you can cast onto a straight, single-pointed needle.

2. Now determine how many needles you'll be using. You can knit using either a set of four or a set of five needles. If you use a set of four, you'll have stitches on three needles and keep one needle free. If you use a set of five, you'll have stitches on four needles and keep one needle free. Unless you can't hold all the stitches on three needles, I suggest you only work with four needles.

3. Now mentally divide the number of stitches by the number of needles holding stitches. For example, if you cast on 60 stitches and are using a set of four needles in which three needles will be active, you know that you need to have 20 stitches on each needle:

   60 (total stitches) ÷ 3 (number of active needles) = 20 (stitches on each needle)

Snarls

In flat knitting, if you twist stitches around the needle, they'll right themselves when you knit the first row. In circular knitting, if you twist stitches around the needle, they'll remain twisted and you'll end up knitting a mobius–type shape that you'll eventually have to rip out and start again. Always make sure your stitches aren't twisted on the circular needle before you begin knitting.

4. Evenly divide the stitches onto the number of active needles.

5. Lay the needles on a flat surface in a triangular shape. If you're using a set of five needles, with four active, lay the needles in a diamond shape. The top of the triangle or diamond should be the two needles that are not yet joined by stitches; this is where you'll begin knitting.

   The tail of the yarn should be on the left side, and the yarn coming from the skein should be on the right. If you're knitting left handed, reverse these instructions.

6. Make sure that the cast-on stitches are all facing inward—toward the middle of the triangle or diamond. Check very carefully to make sure that the cast-on row is straight and that none of the stitches are twisted around the needle.

Getting ready to begin knitting on double-pointed needles.

7. Using the free needle, knit the first stitch from the left side of the triangle. As you knit, pull the yarn fairly tightly; the first stitch joining double-pointed needles is sloppy unless you tug the yarn. You have now joined the circle of knitting.

Knitting the first stitch to join the round.

8. Continue knitting from the stitches on the left needle to the spare needle on the right. When you finish knitting all the stitches on that needle, you'll be holding an empty needle in your left hand.

9. Transfer the spare needle to your right hand and knit all the stitches from the next needle.

10. Keep on knitting each needles' stitches onto the spare needle, knitting round and round. Take special care to knit the first and last stitch of each needle tightly; otherwise, you could end up with a visible "seam" running up the fabric where the needles join.

Pointers

If you're not careful, you can get a stretched-looking line running up the fabric where the needles join. To prevent this problem, knit all the stitches on each needle plus one of the stitches on the next needle onto the spare needle. You then won't have a consistent spot where the needles join, so you won't have a line running up the fabric. If you do this, slip a stitch marker onto the spot where the row begins, just as you would if working on a circular needle.

Pretty neat, isn't it? Now you know how your great-great grandmother made socks for her family!

The tail coming from where the needles were first joined shows you where each row starts (so that you can keep track), but you might want to stick a safety pin at this spot so that you can quickly see where the row begins. Keep moving the safety pin up as the knitted fabric grows.

The Least You Need to Know

➤ Knitting in the round lets you create tubes or flat circles of fabric.

➤ You must use the correct length needle when knitting in the round on a circular needle.

➤ When knitting on double-pointed needles, you need to knit the first and last stitch of each needle tightly to prevent a seam from running up the fabric.

Chapter 12

Making Your Knitting Colorful

In This Chapter

➤ Common colorwork abbreviations

➤ Striping rows

➤ The basics of Fair Isle knitting

➤ Working separate blocks of color using Intarsia knitting

➤ Creating a little knitting deception through duplicate stitch

---

Knitting and color have gone through many trends over the years—from the argyle-knitting craze of the 1950s to the color-splashed pieces that fiber artist Kaffe Fassett introduced in the 1980s. Although working in color is rewarding and often breathtaking, for many knitters it is one of the biggest hurdles to conquer.

Don't let color knitting intimidate you. You can work in multiple colors easily using several different methods. Some methods are as simple as working in a single color. Others are more challenging.

This chapter covers four ways to add color: three knitting techniques and one embroidery embellishment. We'll work through the knitting techniques in what I believe to be the easiest-to-hardest order. You can work your way through each of these methods, getting your feet wet with one technique before moving on to another.

Common Color Abbreviations

The following universal abbreviations will come in handy when you're working in color. For a full list of knit and crochet abbreviations, see the tearcard at the front of this book.

Abbreviation...	What It Means...
alt	Alternate
cc	Contrasting color
col	Color
mc	Main color
rs	Right side
ws	Wrong side

On Your Mark, Get Set, Stripe...

The simplest means of adding color is striping. As you might guess, striping involves changing colors either at the end of a row when flat knitting or at the end of a round when knitting in the round.

To add a stripe, stop knitting with the first color and begin knitting with the second color. A few stitches into the second color, go back and loosely tie the two yarn ends together. That's it.

A couple extra pointers about striping:

➤ If you are working stripes of no more than 6 rows of one color, you don't need to cut the yarn. Instead, you can let the yarn end run from one stripe to another on the back of the fabric.

➤ If you are striping an item such as a scarf or afghan in which both sides will show, do cut the yarn and weave it invisibly into the knitted fabric. Loops of yarn between stripes will show and look messy.

See? Working in color is simple.

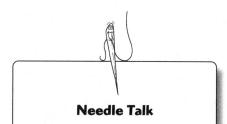

Needle Talk

The *main color* is the predominant color in a multicolor piece; it is abbreviated mc. The *contrasting color* is an accent color used in a piece; it is abbreviated cc. You may have more than one contrasting color.

Needle Talk

Fair Isle knitting is a form of knitting in which two colors are used per row, and the color not in use is carried or stranded along the wrong side of the piece.

Fair Isle Knitting

Traditional Fair Isle knitting is worked with two colors per row. At any time, you are using only one of those colors, so the other color is carried, or stranded, across the back of the piece. For this reason, if you look on the inside of a traditional Fair Isle piece, you'll see that strands of yarn run horizontally across the fabric on the wrong side.

Although Fair Isle patterns feature a burst of many shades of color, they are always created keeping two rules in mind:

➤ Each row uses only two colors, although these two colors can change every few rows.

➤ Each color in a row is used at least every 5 stitches. This guideline keeps the stranded yarn in the back of the piece from becoming unwieldy.

Stranding Yarn from the Right Side

Fair Isle patterns are worked in stockinette stitch, with the knit side being the right side. You keep the stranded yarn on the purl or wrong side. To work a Fair Isle pattern on the right or knit side of your piece, follow these steps:

1. Knit with the first color until you are ready to work with the second color.

2. Let go of the strand of the first color and pick up the strand of the second color.

3. Now knit the next stitch in the second color. Be careful not to pull up the stranded yarn so tightly that the front of the piece puckers; let the stranded yarn rest easily in the back of the piece.

4. When you are finished knitting with the second color and are ready to knit again with the first, gently pull the first color across to the needle point and knit with it. Be careful not to pull up the stranded yarn so tightly that the front of the piece puckers; let it rest easily in the back of the piece.

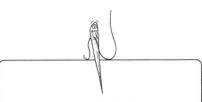

Needle Talk

Stranding means carrying the yarn not currently used for a stitch along the back of a piece, ready to be used. You should not strand yarn for more than 5 stitches at a time, and you should take care to ensure that the stranded yarn isn't left so tight that it puckers the front of the piece.

Snarls

If you will be stranding yarn for more than 5 stitches, you need to use the twist method to prevent yarn from forming large loops—that can snag—on the wrong side of your piece. For details, see the section "Doing the Twist the Fair Isle Way" later in this chapter.

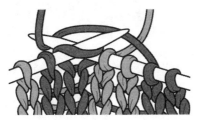

Changing yarn colors from the first color to the second color.

Changing yarn colors from the second color back to the first color.

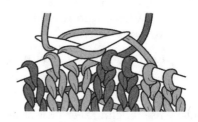

A couple of things to keep in mind when using this method:

➤ Consistently keep one color yarn stranded above the other. In the figures in this section, notice that the second color is always stranded above the first. Let the colors lay easily in place behind the sweater; don't twist them in the back of the piece.

➤ I can't say it enough...don't pull up the strands so tightly in the back that they pucker the front of the sweater. Let them lay gently on the wrong side of the sweater so that the design can lay flat.

Yarn Spinning

Color knitting is frequently associated with Fair Isle Knitting. Legend has it that this form of knitting was brought to the Fair Isles by the shipwrecked sailors of the Spanish Armada in 1588.

Stranding Yarn from the Wrong Side

You purl in Fair Isle almost the same way that you knit. The only difference is that when you're purling, you're facing the stranded yarn. Here's what you do:

1. Purl with the first color until you are ready to work with the second color.

2. Let go of the strand of the first color and pick up the strand of the second color.

3. Now purl the next stitch in the second color. Be careful not to pull up the stranded yarn so tightly that the front of the piece puckers; let the stranded yarn rest easily.

Changing yarn colors from the first color to the second color.

4. When you are finished purling with the second color and ready to purl again with the first, gently pull the first color across to the needle point and purl with it. Be careful not to pull up the stranded yarn so tightly that the front of the piece puckers; let it rest easily in the back of the piece.

As with knitting in Fair Isle, be sure that you don't pull up the yarn too tightly, and be sure that you consistently strand one yarn above the other. In the illustrations in this section, the second color is consistently stranded above the first color.

Changing yarn colors from the second color back to the first color.

Doing the Twist the Fair Isle Way

Suppose you need to strand the yarn for more than 5 stitches? What then? Unless you take a little extra precaution to catch the yarn, you'll end up with cumbersome stranded loops that can catch and pull.

That extra precaution is called twisting. This method is similar to stranding; the only difference, however, is that the yarn is anchored every 3 or 4 stitches by twisting it around the working yarn.

To twist yarn, you literally twist the color you are not using with the color you are using. What you are doing, in essence, is catching the yarn in the back of the piece so that it can be carried more gracefully.

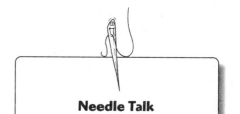

Needle Talk

Twisting is a method of anchoring yarn being carried in the back of your work for more than 5 stitches.

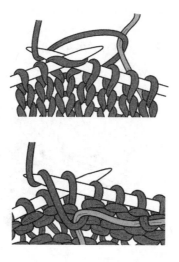

Twisting yarn on the right side.

Twisting yarn on the wrong side.

Snarls

The only time when twisting yarn can create a problem is if you are carrying a dark color behind a light color. In such cases, the twisted yarn can end up slightly showing through on the right side at the place the twist was made. The result is a fabric that doesn't have completely clean, crisp color changes.

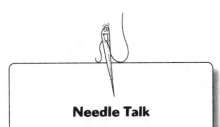

Needle Talk

Intarsia is a type of color knitting in which each block of color is knit from a separate ball or bobbin of yarn.

To prevent a hole in the fabric, wrap yarn strands before beginning a new color block.

Intarsia Knitting

In Intarsia knitting, the yarn is not carried across the back of the work. Instead, a separate ball of yarn—or bobbin of yarn—is used for each block of color in the knitting. Intarsia is the most challenging type of color knitting, but it also produces some of the most spectacular results.

If you will be working with bobbins—which I recommend—wind yarn around the bobbin. Use one bobbin for each block of color. The bobbins can then hang freely from the back of your work, and as you need to use a color, you can unwind the amount that you need.

When it comes time to change yarn colors, on the wrong side of the piece, twist the new color around the old. If you skip this step, you'll have holes in the fabric where the colors change.

Let's start by learning to work Intarsia on the wrong or purl side. You'll begin by having a separate ball of yarn or bobbin for each color block you'll be making. Then follow these steps:

1. Purl with the first color until you are ready to work with the second color.

2. Let go of the strand of the first color. Pick up the strand of the second color.

3. Wrap the strand of the second color around the strand of the first color.

4. Now purl using the second color.

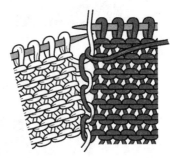

When knitting in Intarsia, you use the same method. The only difference is that you wrap the yarn at the *back* of your work before continuing knitting in a new color.

Pointers

Most color knitting—except stripes—is written in charts. To read the color chart, you work from right to left on odd-numbered rows and from left to right on even-numbered rows. If you are a left-handed knitter, you work from left to right on odd-numbered rows and right to left on even-numbered rows.

Duplicate Stitch

Duplicate stitch is an easy way to add color to your knitwear. A duplicate stitch is exactly what it sounds like: a duplicate of a knitting stitch. You use this stitch to embroider, rather than knit, color patterns into your knitting.

Like Fair Isle and Intarsia, instructions for duplicate stitch are written in color charts; these charts are very much like needlepoint charts. Instead of seeing every square on the pattern as a spot on a canvas, however, view it as a knit stitch you embroider over.

To add duplicate stitch to a finished piece of knitting, follow these steps. If you are working a row of duplicate stitches, you will be working from right to left:

Needle Talk

Kaffe Fassett (pronounced to rhyme with "safe asset") revolutionized the world of knitting with his colorful, fun, and sometimes outrageous patterns. Unlike designers who preceded him and used color conservatively, Mr. Fassett used sweater fabric in much the same way a painter uses a canvas. The result was a welcome jolt to the knitting world. Check out his patterns in the now-classic *Glorious Knits*.

1. Determine where on your knitting you will begin the new pattern. Then thread a yarn needle with a contrasting yarn about 20" long.

2. With right side of work facing you, insert the yarn needle, back to front, into the base of the stitch you will be stitching over. Leave a 3" yarn tail in the back of your work.

119

3. Insert the yarn needle across the back of the stitch being worked, inserting it into the upper-right corner and pulling it out at the upper-left corner.

Working a duplicate stitch.

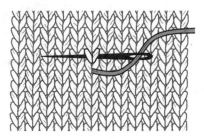

4. Now insert the needle, front to back, into the base of the stitch, where you began the duplicate stitch. You now have a stitch that appears to have been knit in a different color.

   If you will be working the stitch to the left of the one you just knit, insert the needle tip, back to front, into the base of the stitch to the left.

To work duplicate stitch vertically, work the first stitch as you did for the horizontal row. When you are ready to work the second stitch, however, bring the tip of the needle up through the base of the stitch directly above the stitch that you just worked.

When you finish with the duplicate stitch embellishment, weave the ends of the yarn invisibly into the back of the knitted fabric.

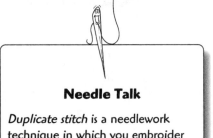

Needle Talk

Duplicate stitch is a needlework technique in which you embroider over knit stitches. The result is a color pattern that appears to be knit in, but is actually embroidered.

Creating a vertical line of duplicate stitch.

The Least You Need to Know

➤ Color knitting often seems intimidating; it is actually very easy.

➤ If you are knitting 5 or fewer rows in a stripe, you don't need to cut the yarn.

➤ If you are going to strand more than 5 stitches, you need to twist the yarn on the wrong side.

➤ Intarsia knitting enables you to knit discrete blocks of color.

➤ You can use duplicate stitch to embroider color patterns on completed knitting pieces.

Chapter 13

Knit Up a Hat in the Round

In This Chapter

➤ The supplies you'll need to get started

➤ Instructions for making a colorful hat that lets you practice working in the round, changing colors, and decreasing

➤ Additional variations and ideas with your basic pattern

The idea of knitting in the round can be intimidating. Granted, you learned what to do in Chapter 11, but reading about a concept and actually doing it are, of course, two different things. Here's a project to get you over the hump. This hat is functional, warm, stylish, and versatile. In addition, while knitting it you can try your hand at working in the round and changing colors, and you'll learn about working different numbers of stitches to accommodate for different sizes.

Feel a cold breeze blowing? Need the proper attire for a snowball fight? Then get out your needles, pick three colors of yarn, and let's get knitting.

What Do I Need?

Because the basic hat has three colors, you can choose colors you love, mixing and matching with abandon. Spend an hour or two in a knit shop and put together as many variations as you like until you find one you adore.

Snarls

Unlike the two previous items you've made, gauge is important with this hat. Be sure to check your gauge or you could end up with a hat so large you resemble Mushmouth from *Fat Albert and the Cosby Kids* or so small it won't fit your Schnauzer.

Snarls

Double-pointed needles can sometimes be hard to navigate, especially the first time you use them, so I suggest that you instead try to find a 16" circular needle. If you opt for the circular needle, you will need to switch to double-pointed needles after you begin decreasing stitches—at whatever point continuing to use the circular needle heavily stretches the fabric. If you do get only double-pointed needles, look for wood, which has a less slick surface than aluminum.

To make the basic hat in either an adult medium (about 18" around, plus some give when stretched) or an adult large (about 20" around, plus some give when stretched), you'll need the following supplies:

➤ Three different colors of bulky yarn:

About 3 ounces (100 yards) of a main color (mc)

About 1 ounce (35 yards) of a contrasting color (A)

About 1 ounce (35 yards) of a second contrasting color (B)

For this sample, I used a teal (main color), black (contrasting color A), and heather gray (contrasting color B). For maximum contrast, you want the mc to be a medium color, A to be a dark color, and B to be a light color.

➤ One set of double-pointed needles in size 8, 9, or 10, and, optionally, one 16" circular needle the same size. I say "about" because you will need to check gauge and make sure that your gauge matches the chapter instructions. Try the size 9 needle first; if your gauge shows too many stitches to the inch, try a size 10. If the size 9 shows too few stitches to the inch, try a size 8.

➤ About 10 stitch markers

➤ A yarn needle for weaving in the ends at the beginning and end of the project

How Do I Make It?

The brim of this hat rolls naturally because it is knit in stockinette stitch; this means that by knitting every stitch, you can create a distinctive design element. (Can you guess how roll-neck sweaters are made? Exactly. You work the neck in stockinette stitch.)

To begin this pattern, swatch the yarn with size 9 needles. If you measure your gauge and find that it's at 4 stitches to the inch, you're ready to begin. If you end up with a different gauge, you'll need to try a different-sized set of needles until the gauge matches 4 stitches to the inch.

Because this pattern shows directions for two different sizes (adult medium and adult large), you might want to read through the pattern and circle the numbers that apply to the size you make. You'll then be able to clearly see which directions to follow.

Gauge: 4 stitches to the inch; be sure to check your gauge.

After you have the right gauge, use the main color (mc) to cast on 72 stitches for an adult medium hat or 80 stitches for an adult large hat. If you are using double-pointed needles, divide these stitches evenly across the needles. (Remember to keep one needle free to work the stitches.)

Place a stitch marker right before the first stitch you are about to knit. Now join the round, being very careful not to twist the stitches. (If you need help with this step, refer to Chapter 11.)

Follow these steps to knit the hat:

1. Knit $2^1/_2$" in the main color for a medium hat or 3" for a large hat.

2. Change to color A and knit 2 rounds.

3. Change to color B and knit 6 rounds.

4. Change back to color A and knit 2 more rounds.

5. Change to mc and continue knitting. For the medium-sized hat, knit until you have $6^1/_2$" total from the beginning row. For the large-sized hat, knit until you have 7" total from the beginning row.

Snarls

When you're knitting with a set of double-pointed needles (as opposed to one circular needle), you can very easily accidentally pick up "extra" stitches at the end of the needle. Watch your first several rounds carefully and count the number of stitches on each needle as you finish with each needle.

6. Now you begin decreasing. To do so, knit 6 stitches, knit 2 stitches together, and slide a marker onto the needle.

   Complete this step 9 times total for the medium hat or 10 times total for the large hat. If you're making the medium hat, you now have 64 stitches on the needle(s); if you're making the large hat, you now have 72 stitches on the needle(s).

7. Knit 1 round.

8. Knit to 2 stitches before the first marker, knit 2 stitches together. Slide the marker to the right-hand needle.

   If you're making the medium hat, complete this step a total of 9 times. If you're making the large hat, complete this step a total of 10 times.

9. Repeat steps 7 and 8 until you have only 2 stitches between each marker.

   If you are using a circular needle, at some point the stitches will begin to stretch to accommodate the needle. At that point, you need to switch to using double-pointed needles.

   If you're making the medium hat, you now have 18 stitches total on the needle(s); if you're making the large hat, you have 20 stitches total on the needle(s).

10. Knit 1 round.

11. Knit 2 stitches together. Repeat this step across the row, simultaneously removing the stitch markers from the needle. (They no longer serve any purpose.)

    If you're making the medium hat, you now have 9 stitches on the needle(s). If you're making the large hat, you now have 10 stitches on the needle(s).

12. If you're making the medium hat, knit 1; then knit 2 stitches together 4 times. You now have 5 stitches on the needle.

    If you're making the large hat, knit 2 stitches together 5 times. You now have 5 stitches on the needle.

13. Break off the yarn, thread a yarn needle, and run the needle through the stitches remaining on your knitting needles. Draw up this yarn so that you close the hole in the top of the hat.

To finish, use a yarn needle to weave all yarn ends into the fabric of the inside of the hat.

Variations on a Theme

Want to stray from the beaten path? Try some of these modifications:

➤ Make a cuffed edge rather than a rolled one. To do this, work the first 2^1/$_2$" in knit 2, purl 2 ribbing. Then purl 1 row to make a turning point; when you wear the hat, you'll fold the cuff up at this point. Then continue knitting. Because the cuff obscures the original stripe, why not knit the ribbed cuff in one color and the rest of the hat in another?

➤ Add a pom-pom to the top, using all three colors from the hat.

➤ Make the hat for a baby. To do so, use double-knitting weight yarn. You'll need 1^1/$_2$ ounces main color, ^{1}/$_2$ ounce contrasting color A, and 1 ounce contrasting color B. Use size 5 needles (or the size necessary to get a gauge of 5 stitches to the inch); if you are beginning on a circular needle, use a 16" needle. Cast on 72 stitches for a 6-month-old size and 80 stitches for about a 1-year-old size. When you've knit 2", add the stripe. Begin decreasing at 4" for a small size and 4^1/$_4$" for a larger size. Shape in exactly the same way as the adult size.

The Least You Need to Know

➤ Knitting in the round isn't difficult once you get the hang of it.

➤ Changing needle size and yarn thickness, you can change some adult-sized items into baby sizes.

➤ When making items such as clothing, carefully checking gauge is very important.

Chapter 14

Talking the Talk: Reading a Knit Pattern

In This Chapter

➤ Deciphering common knit abbreviations

➤ Working with the language of repeats

➤ Reading charts rather than words

➤ Cracking the sizing code

Open a book of knitting patterns, and your memories might take you back to child-hood games where you drew treasure maps written in a secret code known only to your best friends. *k1, p2, sl st, k2Tog, psso.* Does this tell you how to make a sweater or where to find the chest of gold?

Because longhand knitting patterns would be cumbersome to write and inefficient to read, a standard pattern-writing abbreviated language was devised. This language enables you to work through and understand patterns more quickly, and to carry a pattern for a complex Aran sweater on a single sheet of paper rather than in a novel-sized book. Like your secret backyard language, however, unless you know the code, you can't read the pattern.

After you finish reading this chapter, you'll be able to decipher abbreviations, repeats, and even wordless patterns.

Common Knit Abbreviations

Most common knit terms have a universal abbreviation. In almost every pattern you read, these abbreviations allow complex patterns to be written quickly and cleanly. As you'll find when you begin knitting more frequently, this abbreviation system actually makes patterns less cumbersome to read and follow.

Abbreviation	Full Name
alt	Alternate
approx	Approximately
beg	Begin(ing)
bet	Between
bo	Bind off
cc	Contrasting color
c4b	cable 4 back
c4f	cable 4 front
col	Color
cont	Continue(ing)
dbl	Double
dec	Decrease(ing)
dpn	Double pointed
fin	Finished
foll	Following
g or gr	Gram(s)
in(s)	Inch(es)
inc	Increase(ing)
k	Knit
k2Tog	Knit two together
kbl	Knit through back of loop
kwise	Knitwise
lp(s)	Loop(s)
mc	Main color
med	Medium
mm	Millimeter
m1	Make 1
mult	Multiple
opp	Opposite
oz	Ounces
p	Purl
p2Tog	Purl two together
pat(s)	Pattern(s)
pm	Place marker
p tbl	Purl through back of loop
psso	Pass slip stitch over
pwise	Purlwise
rem	Remaining

Abbreviation	Full Name
rep	Repeat
rev st st	Reverse stockinette stitch
rib	Ribbing
rnd(s)	Round(s)
rs	Right side
sc	Single crochet
sk	Skip
sl	Slip
sl st	Slip stitch
sp(s)	Space(s)
ssk	Slip slip knit
st(s)	Stitch(es)
st st	Stockinette stitch
tbl	Through back of loop
tog	Together
ws	Wrong side
wyib	With yarn in back
wyif	With yarn in front
yb	Yarn back
yf	Yarn forward
yo	Yarn over
ytb	Yarn to back
ytf	Yarn to front

And Asterisks for All!

When you first glance at a knit pattern, you'll initially adjust your glasses and get ready to write an angry letter to the publisher. With so many weird symbols, it looks like a computer program gone awry.

Amazingly, these patterns are created using standardized symbols written in conjunction with the knit abbreviations. The system *does* make sense. If you need help, refer to the list of knit abbreviations.

The Asterisk Makes Its Mark

Asterisks play a crucial role in knit patterns. They indicate the start of a section that you will repeat.

When you see any of these asterisk combinations, it means *repeat from*:

*

**

***

In other words, You need to repeat the instructions following the *, **, or *** as many times as given. You would first work the information given once. Then you would repeat that information as many times as specified.

Here's an example:

*k2Tog, yo. Repeat from * to end of row.

This pattern is telling you to knit 2 stitches together and then do a yarn over. You then repeat these two procedures all the way across the rest of the row.

Parenthetical Considerations

Parentheses work in much the same way as asterisks. When you see this

( )

it means *work what is in the parentheses as many times as given*. Here's an example:

(p2, kbl, p1) 3 times

This means that you should purl 2, knit to the back of the loop in the next stitch, and purl 1 a total of 3 times.

Plus a Couple Extra Knit Stitches...

Plus signs indicate that you should repeat something between the plus signs. When you see

+ to +

it means *work the instructions between the plus signs and repeat as many times as specified*. Here's an example:

+p1, k2Tog, p1+. Repeat + to + 5 more times.

This means you would purl 1, knit 2 together, and purl 1; you would then repeat this sequence five more times.

Pointers

Reading PatternSpeak becomes easier when you really start to work from a pattern. If you're initially confused about what the instructions are saying, write them out in longhand and work through them step by step. This method might take a little extra time, but it will help you get used to reading patterns. In addition, it might save you the time and heartbreak of ripping out and re-doing your work.

Charting the Patterns

Recently, patterns have been written more in charted symbols than in written words. These symbols show either changes in the stitching, such as changing from knitting to purling or adding a cable, or they show changes in color. This strategy has several advantages:

➤ Charted patterns enable you to easily see where you are in a pattern and help ensure that you are on the right track. With a visual pattern, you can somewhat compare the pattern with your knitted fabric. If the two match, you're okay. If not, you might need to look at the pattern again.

Pointers

As a help when reading charted patterns, place a Post-It note on the pattern so that it aligns with the bottom of the row you're currently working. Each time you finish a row, move the paper up one row on the chart. If the phone rings and you get into a long conversation with a window salesman, you'll be able to come back to your knitting without spending 15 minutes figuring out which row you were on.

➤ Charted patterns generally contain fewer printed errors. No one's perfect, and knitted patterns *can* contain typos and other errors. Just as you can verify your work against the pattern, so can the author. If written instructions are incorrect, the mistakes can sometimes go unnoticed. Patterns can all too easily be printed with typos such as "k3" rather than "k2." In the middle of a complex series of instructions, this seemingly simple mistake can cause even the most stoic knitter to break down. It's much harder, however, to print a chart incorrectly; if the pattern in the printed chart doesn't resemble what it's supposed to resemble, the author can generally see immediately that something is amiss.

➤ Once you get the hang of it, charted patterns are easy to follow—for many people, easier than written patterns.

Take a look at this pattern for a 10-stitch cable pattern:

Charted patterns often make working in complex patterns easier.

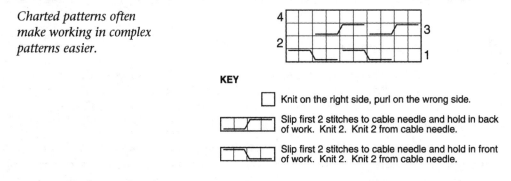

To read the pattern, work the odd rows from right to left and the even rows from left to right.

For this pattern, start the first row in the lower-right corner, and follow row 1 from right to left, row 2 from left to right, and so on. If you are a left-handed knitter, reverse this: Read odd rows from left to right and even rows from right to left.

Here's how the pattern would look if written out:

Row 1: K2, c4f twice.

Row 2: P across.

Row 3: C4b twice, k2.

Row 4: P across.

Can you seen how looking at the chart might give you a better idea of where your stitches will fall?

Calling All Sizes

Knitting patterns have one more unique attribute that you need to understand. Because sweater patterns are made to be adaptable to both your petite little sister and your oversized Uncle Fred, they are written with the variations for each size included. These variations are typically included in parentheses.

A pattern, for example, might begin like this:

To fit chest size 34" (36", 38", 40", 42")

This means that the entire pattern is written using this same parenthetical annotation for larger sizes. If you are making the 36" size, then, for any shaping or patterning instructions you will always follow the first number in the parentheses. For example, as you're shaping the armhole, you might see the following:

bo 6 (8, 9, 10, 12) st at beg of next row.

You would then bind off 8 stitches—the first number in the parentheses. Follow this same system throughout the pattern.

Snarls

This parenthetical annotation system is wonderful for writing lots of instructions compactly, but it can be hazardous if you're not paying close attention. To avoid accidentally following the wrong sizing instructions, before you start knitting, go through the pattern and circle the instructions for the size that you will be knitting. You then can easily see the numbers you need to follow.

The Least You Need to Know

➤ Universal abbreviations mean that patterns can be read and written more quickly and effectively.

➤ Asterisks, parentheses, and plus signs are used to indicate repeats in a pattern.

➤ Charted patterns enable you to verify your stitches by comparing the knitted fabric with the chart.

➤ Patterns often come with various sizes written into the pattern; you follow the number that aligns with the size you want to make.

Chapter 15

Correcting Common Knitting Gaffes

In This Chapter

➤ Stopping mistakes before they happen

➤ Turning twisted stitches

➤ Catching dropped stitches

➤ Correcting sloppy stitches

➤ Letting 'er rip

We all make mistakes. Even in knitting, one of the most relaxing and enjoyable of pursuits, mistakes occur that can dampen your enthusiasm for the craft.

Fortunately, most knitting *faux pas* are minor and easily correctable. This chapter walks you through the best ways to prevent the most common mistakes, teaches you what to do when a mistake occurs, and helps you determine when it's time to forget correcting and just start over.

As you learn any new craft, you need to feel comfortable and in control. Don't be afraid to make or to correct mistakes.

Taking the Bull by the Horns: Preventing Mistakes

Some of the most common knitting errors are due to not watching what you're doing. As you become adept at knitting, you won't even have to look at your knitting to know something's gone awry. Instead, your hands will know what to feel for as you're flying across each row, and they'll stop you when something's amiss.

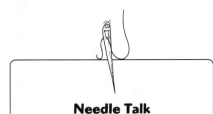

Yarn Spinning

During World War I, American citizens were asked to knit socks for the soldiers fighting in Europe. Several knitting bees in New York City's Central Park drew thousands of men, women, and children, all clicking needles in unison, working to clothe the troops.

Needle Talk

Twisted stitches are stitches twisted on your needle. Because the knitted loops are twisted, the stitches are tighter than correctly knit stitches and don't open when stretched.

When you're first learning to knit, however, you have to be much more conscious of what your hands are doing. You can usually avoid the two common mistakes—dropped stitches and adding stitches—if you watch your hands as you knit.

In addition, count the stitches after every completed row. Sure, this exercise seems tedious, but you'll immediately know whether you lost or added a stitch. You can then look over the row, one stitch at a time. Check to see whether a stitch has been dropped from the needle or whether the needle contains a loop of yarn that isn't part of a stitch.

Turning Twisted Stitches

"Twisted stitches" sounds like the name of an '80s rock band, doesn't it?

In knitting, twisted stitches are exactly what the name says: stitches that get twisted on your needle. You generally get twisted stitches one of two ways: by knitting into the front, rather than the back, of the needle, or by incorrectly unraveling stitches (which you'll learn about later in this chapter).

To correct twisted stitches, use the point of the needle that the stitch isn't on to slide the stitch off the needle. Untwist it, and place it back on the needle.

Pointers

If you feel fairly comfortable with knitting, you can correct twisted stitches by the way you insert your needle while you are working. To correct a stitch, knit or purl through the back loop on a twisted stitch.

Untwisting a twisted stitch.

Catching Dropped Stitches

Probably the most common mistake in knitting is losing a stitch. You start out with 20 stitches on your needle and after a period of time, you find you have only 19.

Being an optimist, you might shrug and decide to just add back a couple stitches and be on your way. Trouble is, a dropped stitch has a tendency to run. Think of what pantyhose do when they get a small hole; your knitted items will do the same. Now think how wonderful it would be if you could close up the pantyhose hole before it ran. When you're knitting, you can.

Using Needles to Pick Up a Dropped Knit Stitch

Let's say you're working in stockinette stitch (knit 1 row, purl 1 row) and notice you have a dropped stitch in the row below. What now? Fortunately, you can use your knitting needles to salvage the stitch before it runs farther down the knitted piece. Here's all you do:

1. From the front (right side) of your work, knit across the row to the position of the dropped stitch.

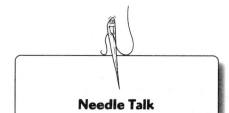

Needle Talk

Dropped stitches are stitches that accidentally slide off the needle during knitting. If left unfixed, dropped stitches can run down through the knitted fabric.

Yarn Spinning

Some patterns call for you to drop stitches intentionally. First, you knit an entire piece. On the last row, you drop specific stitches—maybe every tenth stitch. The result is a lace-like pattern running vertically through the piece.

139

*Locate the dropped stitch
and knit to it.*

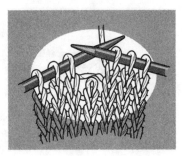

2. Insert the right-hand needle, from front to back, into both the loop of the dropped stitch and the horizontal strand of yarn in the row above the dropped stitch. Make sure that the strand is positioned left of the stitch on the needle.

*Insert the needle into the
dropped stitch and the line
of yarn above the stitch.*

3. Insert the left-hand needle, back to front, into the loop of the dropped stitch. Then lift the loop over the strand of yarn on the needle. This action is just like binding off a stitch. Now the corrected stitch is on the right-hand needle.

*Pass the dropped stitch
over the horizontal bar of
yarn.*

4. Slip the corrected stitch from the right-hand needle to the left-hand needle.

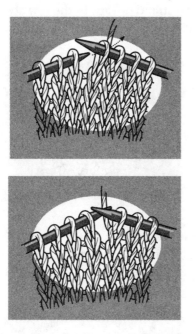

Move the stitch to the left-hand needle and keep on knitting.

Knit away. The dropped stitch is now history; let us never speak of it again.

Using Needles to Pick Up a Dropped Purl Stitch

Picking up a purl stitch is a lot like picking up a knit stitch; you just need to reverse a few things. Here's how:

1. Purl across the row to the position of the dropped stitch.

Locate the dropped stitch and purl to it.

2. Insert the right-hand needle, from front to back, into both the loop of the dropped stitch and the horizontal strand of yarn in the row above the dropped stitch. Make sure that the strand is positioned left of the stitch on the needle.

Insert the needle into the dropped stitch and the line of yarn above the stitch.

3. Insert the left-hand needle, from back to front, into the loop of the dropped stitch. Then lift the loop over the strand of yarn on the needle. This action is just like binding off a stitch. Now the corrected stitch is on the right-hand needle.

Pass the dropped stitch over the horizontal bar of yarn.

4. Slip the corrected stitch from the right-hand needle to the left-hand needle.

Move the stitch to the left-hand needle and keep on purlin'.

That's all there is to it.

How to Become a Major Pick-Up Artist

At times, a dropped stitch goes unnoticed for several rows before you discover that you have a problem. When you notice the mistake, attach a safety pin just under the dropped stitch so that you can identify the area.

Although you can use a knitting needle and laboriously follow the stitch-saving steps in the previous sections, you'll find the work goes much faster with a crochet hook.

To pick up the stitches, insert the crochet hook, front to back, into the dropped stitch. Now use the hook to catch the horizontal line of yarn above the dropped stitch, and pull this yarn through the stitch. Continue working the stitch up the "ladder" of yarn until you get to the end.

Yarn Spinning

Writer Dorothy Parker was an avid knitter whose projects accompanied her *everywhere*. During Hollywood's heyday, Dorothy and her husband, Alan Campbell, co-wrote award-winning screenplays for large film studios. Their writing method was simple and effective: After Alan blocked out the scenes, Dorothy sat in a corner, knitting and spouting brilliant dialog, while Alan typed up her words.

Using a crochet hook to work a dropped stitch up the "ladder."

To pick up stitches when purling, follow the same steps as for knitting, but insert the hook back to front.

To pick up a dropped stitch when working garter stitch (knit every row), alternate the knitting and purling instructions. Make sure that you use the knitting technique when the row is smooth and the purling technique when the row is bumpy.

Using a crochet hook to fix a dropped stitch on a garter stitch piece.

Showing Sloppy Stitches Who's Boss

At some point, you're going to stop knitting, hold up your piece admirably, and notice a hole in the middle. You've checked; it's not a dropped stitch. It's just a much larger (shall we dare say sloppier) stitch than the others in the piece. What to do?

Simple. Grab your spare knitting needle and gently poke into the stitches surrounding the larger stitch. You're trying to slightly stretch those stitches to take up yarn and even out all the stitches. After a minute or so of adjusting surrounding stitches, you'll never know the larger stitch was there.

When All Else Fails: Let 'Er Rip!

Some mistakes are just too time-consuming or too impossible to fix. Suppose, for example, that you're working a cable and find one row where you forgot to work the pattern. If you can live with it, do. If you determine that you'll always feel inferior when you look at the product, get ready to learn the fine art of unraveling.

Taking Out Just a Few Stitches

If the area you need to unravel to is one row or fewer of stitches, you'll want to pull the stitches out one stitch at a time.

To unravel stitches one at a time, follow these steps:

1. Slide the first stitch off the right-hand needle.

2. Gently tug the yarn that "feeds" into your knitting to unravel the stitch.

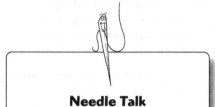

Needle Talk

Ripping out means unraveling or pulling out stitches. You rip out when you find that you don't like the look or size of the knitted fabric, or when you find a mistake that you need to undo.

Snarls

If you don't insert an unraveled stitch onto the needle correctly, you'll wind up with a twisted stitch. Be sure that when you place an unraveled stitch on the left-hand needle, the part of the loop in front of the needle leans toward the right.

3. Place the remaining stitch onto the left-hand needle. Be sure to insert the needle into the middle of the loop.

Unraveling knit stitches one by one.

Unraveling purl stitches one by one.

Going Wild!

Let's say that the mistake isn't three stitches down the needle but three inches down the knitted fabric. Heartbreaking as undoing work can be, you're about to be introduced to the most cathartic move in knitting: ripping out stitches.

To unravel several rows of stitches, first use a safety pin to mark the offending row. Then slide the knitting off the needles and pull the yarn with wild abandon. Feels good, doesn't it?

When you get down to one row above the problem row, slow down. Use the procedure in the preceding section to, one-by-one, unravel the stitches and place them back on the needle.

Snarls

To avoid an extra stitch at the beginning of a row, make sure your yarn is at the *back* of your work when you start a knit row and in the *front* of your work when you start a purl row.

Yarn Spinning

The members of the electronic KnitList on the Internet have their own words for ripping out stitches. *Tink* refers to taking out stitches one at a time; *tink* is *knit* backward. *Frog* refers to ripping out large batches of knitting; they claim that "rip it! rip it!" sounds like "ribbit! ribbit!"

Wind the unraveled thread back on your ball, take a deep breath, and proceed.

Extra, Extra!

Another common knitting gaff is to end up with too many stitches on a row. If you find one row a bit hefty, look carefully at your work to identify the problem. Then mark the trouble spot with a safety pin. Chances are, you grabbed an extra loop of yarn and didn't notice the problem until you had knit several rows.

To correct the mistake, unravel your work to the problem stitch. Unravel that stitch. Count the stitches to make sure the number is correct. Go grab a cup of tea, and come back to your knitting.

The Least You Need to Know

➤ Mistakes don't have to frighten you away from knitting—many are either avoidable or easily fixable.

➤ You can use a crochet hook to catch stitches that you dropped several rows back.

➤ You can disguise a too-big stitch by evening out the stitches around it.

➤ Unraveling great loads of knitting can be terribly cathartic.

Part 4
Crochet Basics

The best buddy of knitting is crocheting: another craft that is predominantly a matter of connecting loops. In this section, you learn how to prepare to crochet, how to accomplish the basic steps, and how to jazz up your work with color and shaping. In addition, you learn how to read those crazy, abbreviated crochet patterns.

If you're ready to try your new skills, whip up a fabulous and fast afghan or make a set of neat woven placemats. All the instructions are in this section.

Chapter 16

An Overview of Crochet Tools

In This Chapter

➤ Understanding the anatomy of a crochet hook

➤ Unscrambling the various needle sizes

➤ Additional accessories that will enhance your crocheting

Crocheting requires two basic supplies: yarn and a crochet hook. You learned about your yarn options in Chapter 2; now it's time to learn about crochet hooks. I'll also cover some of the other available tools that can make your crocheting easier.

Crochet Hooks

Crochet hooks come in sizes so small that you can only feel the point with your fingertip and so large they look as though they could double as boat anchors. As you'd expect, they also come in every size in between.

For every yarn on the market, there is a *suggested* hook size to use with it. Despite the suggestions, however, you won't find a scientific formula for combining hook size and yarn weight. Because each individual project is designed with a specific look in mind, you might find yourself crocheting cotton thread with a large needle or working worsted-weight cotton with a small one. In addition, crocheters differ in how tightly or loosely they crochet, which makes it even more difficult to come up with a set formula.

Pointers

The most important concept you can learn in your hook-size selection is gauge: how many stitches you need to crochet to make an inch. Gauge varies based on the type yarn you select, the size hook you use, and how tightly or loosely you crochet. If you're feeling woozy by all this talk, flip back to Chapter 2 for a refresher on gauge.

Parts of a Crochet Hook

Before I go into crochet hook sizes, let's take a look at what a crochet hook really looks like and what each part is named.

The humble crochet hook is actually made up of four distinct parts.

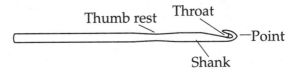

Thumb rest   Throat   —Point   Shank

Yarn Spinning

During the mid-nineteenth century, the noble ladies of England had time on their hands and an interest in finding a hobby. They turned to crochet. As you might expect, the craft experienced a surge in popularity at this time.

Each part of the hook has a unique function:

➤ The *point* goes into the stitch on the crocheted fabric.

➤ The *throat* catches the yarn. The throat needs to be large enough to accommodate the yarn being used.

➤ The *shank* holds the loops with which you're working. The shank is really what determines the size of your stitches.

➤ The *thumb rest* is just that—a place to rest your thumb so that you can rotate the hook with ease while working.

These four simple parts have been designed for comfort and to help speed your work.

Reverting to Type: Crochet Hook Sizes and Types

Crochet hooks come in different sizes—and different materials. The material used to make the hook corresponds with the hook's size.

Steel hooks are the smallest: Some are so fine you might mistake them for darning needles. Next in size are aluminum and plastic hooks. In addition, some wooden hooks are available in larger sizes. The average length of a crochet hook is about 6 inches.

Here's where things get tricky. Crochet hooks are sized according to three different systems: U.S., English, and Continental. Each system uses a different numbering or lettering system to indicate size. As a result, a new crocheter not familiar with the differences in these three types can become puzzled fairly quickly.

To simplify it all, earmark this page. You'll want to refer often to the charts that follow.

U.S.	1	2	3	4	5	6	7	8	9	10	11	12	13	14
English	3/0	2/0	1/0	1	1 1/2	2	2 1/2	3	4	5	5 1/2	6	6 1/2	7
Continental Rim	3	2.5		2		1.75	1.5	1.25	1	0.75		0.6		

Sizing chart for steel crochet hooks.

U.S.	1/B	2/C	3/D	4/E	5/F	6/G	8/H	9/I	10/J	10 1/2 /K
English	12	11	10	9	8	7	6	5	4	2
Continental Rim	2 1/2	3		3 1/2	4	4 1/2	5	5 1/2	6	7

Sizing chart for aluminum and plastic crochet hooks.

Although crochet hook sizing and the wide variety of hook options might seem intimidating, it can also work to your advantage. If you buy a larger size hook and experience some difficulties with the hook and the yarn, try the same size in another material. For example, you might find you prefer wood to aluminum. In addition, try a hook with a differently shaped point—perhaps one that's more round than sharply angled. With some practice, you'll find the type hook you prefer, and you'll use this type for all your projects.

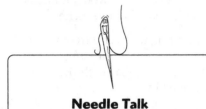

Needle Talk

Afghan (Tunisian) crochet is a special type of crochet that requires the crocheter to hold many stitches on the crochet hook. Special afghan hooks that look like a cross between a crochet hook and a knitting needle are available for this purpose.

Afghan Hooks

One type of specialized crochet—called Afghan or Tunisian crochet—requires you to hold many stitches on the hook simultaneously. Obviously, if the average length of a crochet hook is 6 inches, you'd run out of room quickly on a regular crochet hook. As you might expect, specialized tools were created to make a crocheter's life easier.

Afghan hooks are much longer than regular crochet hooks; they come in three lengths: 9", 14", and 20". In addition, the hooks have a cap or knob on the opposite end from the hook; this knob serves the same purpose as the knob at the end of a knitting needle: It keeps stitches from falling off the end. (If you're curious about Afghan crochet, turn to Chapter 22 for a sneak preview.)

Afghan hooks enable you to work Afghan crochet without incident.

Now you can even find Afghan hooks that have a long flexible cord on one end. These cords hold many stitches, and the flexibility of the cord means that your work can more easily rest in your lap.

Flexible Afghan hooks make Afghan crochet even easier.

Extra! Extra! Additional Crocheting Accessories

Although all you *need* to crochet is a hook and some yarn, a few additional accessories will prove invaluable as you begin making projects of your own.

Measuring Tools

The most important accessory is a good tape measure or a gauge counter. As you learned in Chapter 3, accurate gauge is often crucial in crocheting, and good measuring tools are crucial to accurate gauge. In addition, you'll use the tape measure for a million different measuring tasks: cutting fringe, counting a number of inches on a sweater front before shaping for armholes, verifying the size of the crocheted placemats, and so on.

Bobbins

Bobbins are helpful accessories to have on hand when you're working in multiple colors. These little gems are made of plastic and are easy to find in yarn shops. Bobbins look similar to bread-bag tabs, only larger. To use a bobbin, wrap yarn around it and crochet from the bobbin, rather than from a ball of yarn. You can then unwind only what you need for the next few stitches, and you won't have to negotiate cumbersome amounts of yarn.

If you're feeling ambitious, you can make your own bobbins out of cardboard. Just follow the shape of the illustration of any of the bobbins on this page.

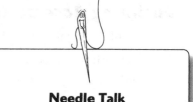

Needle Talk

Bobbins are plastic tabs that hold small amounts of yarn. They are invaluable when working on pieces that have many color changes.

Bobbins let you work in multiple colors without creating a tangled mess of yarn.

Stitch Markers

Stitch markers are also handy. When you work certain patterns you need to keep track of information such as where to increase or when to repeat a particular stitch pattern. To use stitch markers, you affix them to the crocheted fabric. If you don't want to purchase another accessory, just use a safety pin.

Stitch markers

Finishing Accessories

Needles and pins...hey! That might make a catchy tune.

To finish your pieces, you'll need some needles and pins—at least one needle and a few pins.

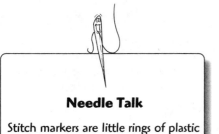

> **Needle Talk**
>
> Stitch markers are little rings of plastic you use to mark a specific spot in a piece.

You'll use the pins to hold your work together for sewing seams and for blocking pieces. (To learn about blocking and finishing your work, take a look at Chapter 24.) In a pinch, you can also use straight pins as stitch markers, but I don't recommend it; inadvertently finding a pinpoint is jolting.

Yarn needles, which have dull rather than sharp points, enable you to weave in yarn ends and sew together seams. These needles come in varying sizes to accommodate different thicknesses of yarn.

Needles and pins enable you to finish your pieces in style.

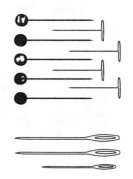

The Least You Need to Know

➤ Crochet hooks come in three varieties—U.S., English, and Continental—and each uses a different sizing scheme.

➤ Crochet hooks are made from different products (wood, aluminum, steel, and plastic) and with differing point shapes. You can experiment to find the shape and material you like best.

➤ A couple of accessories such as bobbins and yarn needles will enhance your crocheting.

Chapter 17

Getting Started: Basic Crochet Stitches

In This Chapter

➤ Getting ready to start hooking

➤ First things first: making a foundation chain

➤ Practicing the basic stitches

➤ Left-handed crochet principles

Crocheting is a lot of fun. You can watch your hands transform a hook and a ball of string into something exquisite.

The step-by-step, hand-by-hand illustrations in the pages that follow will make it easy to learn how to crochet. By the time you finish this chapter, with crochet hook comfortably in hand, you'll be able to make a slip knot and a chain, work slip stitches, and perform stitches with ease. These skills are the foundation of all basic crochet.

And if you're a southpaw, you won't be left out. We've put together and illustrated an entire left-handed section.

So get out the yarn. Pick up your crochet hook. Sit down, and let's get going.

Common Basic Crochet Abbreviations

The following abbreviations are commonly used in crochet patterns. For a full list of knit and crochet abbreviations, see the tearcard at the front of this book.

Abbreviation...	What It Means...
ch st	Chain stitch
dc	Double crochet
hdc	Half-double crochet
sc	Single crochet
sl st	Slip stitch
trc	Triple crochet
yo	Yarn over

The following sections explain the meaning of all this mumbo jumbo.

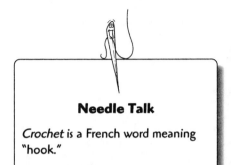

Needle Talk

Crochet is a French word meaning "hook."

Basic Training

Like all needlecrafts, crochet begins with getting a proper grip on your tools. There are two easy ways to hold a crochet hook. Try them and decide which feels best for you.

Practice each of these simple grips. You'll find one of the positions to be the more comfortable. Be prepared to switch positions, though. You won't know how they really feel until you actually start to crochet.

You can hold the hook one of two ways. Either position and lightly grip your hook in your hand as you would hold a pencil, or hold the hook how you would grip a spoon when stirring something thick.

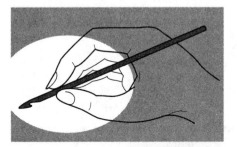

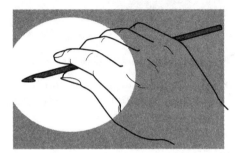

Slip Knot in the Making

With the crochet hook comfortably in your hand you're ready to begin working with the yarn. First, make a slip knot and attach the yarn to your hook. Here's a simple three-step way to tie the slip knot.

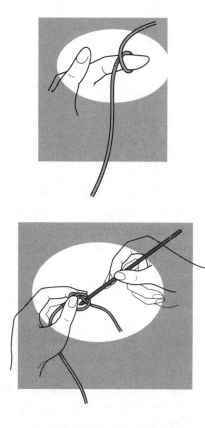

Loop the yarn around your left index finger.

Slip the yarn from your finger and hold the loop between your thumb and index finger.

Use the crochet hook, held in your right hand, to draw the loop up and around the hook.

Finally, gently pull each of the ends in opposite directions. This tightens the knot and makes it smaller. It's that simple!

Pointers

When is a knot not a stitch? When it's a loop formed by the slip knot on the crochet hook. Although it looks like a stitch, it never counts as a stitch. It is simply a way to attach the yarn securely to the hook. The only exception to the rule is when you are working in Afghan crochet (which is explained in Chapter 22).

Needle Talk

A *slip knot* is a knot that slips easily along the cord around which it is tied. Also called a "running knot," it is the most widely used knot for making a noose—but stick to using it for crocheting!

The Whole Yarn in Your Hands

Now that you've made a slip knot and secured the yarn to the hook, you'll want to practice holding the yarn. The techniques in this section let you control how the yarn is "fed" into your work.

Take the yarn with your left hand. With the palm of your left hand facing up, thread the yarn through your fingers.

Practice holding the yarn so that it can flow through your fingers. Moving your index finger up and down lets you increase or decrease the tautness of the yarn. You'll begin to find a rhythm as you start to work, and soon the movement will feel very natural. To get ready to crochet, follow these instructions:

Grasp the yarn between your ring and little finger, 4 inches or so from the hook.

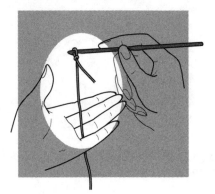

Pointers

How you hold the yarn is an individual choice. However, it's important that you're not only comfortable with the yarn, but also that you have control over it. Hold the yarn taut enough to be able to "hook" (catch) the yarn with the barb of the crochet hook, but not so tightly that you can't get the hook through your stitches. With practice, you'll get a feel for tension.

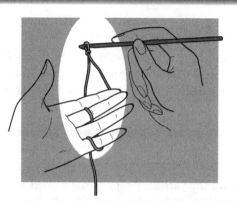

Draw the yarn toward you—from your little and ring fingers—threaded over your middle finger and leading under your index finger.

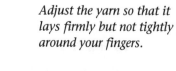

Adjust the yarn so that it lays firmly but not tightly around your fingers.

One more fundamental before I move on: catching the yarn. This movement, catching the yarn with your hook, is called a yarn over, abbreviated yo. The hook is under the yarn, the yarn is over the hook. Your index finger comes into play here, because each time you catch the yarn with your hook, you guide the yarn by moving your index finger up and down.

To do a yarn over, pass the hook under and over the yarn from back to front.

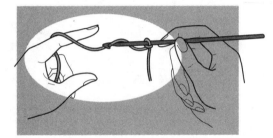

Pointers

Not all techniques are easy for everyone. Here's an alternative if you're having trouble "wrapping" the yarn around all your fingers: Instead of wrapping the yarn, let it flow behind your index finger, in front of your middle and ring fingers, and back behind your little finger.

Needle Talk

A *yarn over* is the movement of passing the hook under the yarn and then catching the yarn with the hook. This movement is fundamental to crochet. In crochet instructions, a yarn over is abbreviated *yo*.

You've now attached the yarn to the hook, you're holding the yarn in your left hand, and you've accomplished the yarn over movement. It's time to crochet.

The Base of All Crochet: The Foundation Chain

If you were constructing a building, you would need to start with a solid foundation. Crocheting is no different. The start is comprised of a *foundation chain*. It is this base that holds your stitches and all succeeding rows. The next section shows you how to build a foundation chain.

Making the Chain

The illustrations that follow walk you through the process for making a foundation chain. Initially, this technique can be tricky. Just practice. It'll become natural.

Now, make another chain stitch, and then another, and another. As you work, keep moving your thumb up and hold the yarn right below your hook. This movement becomes second nature as you practice.

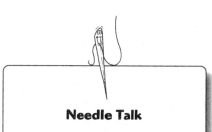

Needle Talk

The *foundation chain* is a chain-stitched row that stands as the base of your crocheting—the foundation from which a piece is built.

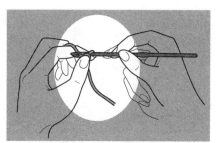

To start a chain, grasp the short end of the yarn, right below the slip knot.

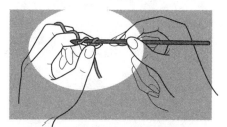

With your crochet hook, catch the yarn that's between your thumb and index finger by going under the yarn. Then pull the hook through the slip loop on your hook. You just made your first chain stitch.

Making a row of chain stitches.

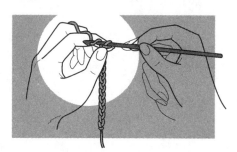

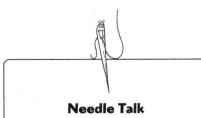

Needle Talk

A *chain stitch* is made when you catch the yarn with the hook and draw the yarn through the loop on the hook. A chain stitch is abbreviated in instructions as *ch st.*

Now chain on. The more you practice making chain stitches, the more natural the movement will become for you.

Heads or Tails?

It's important to recognize the chain's front from its back. Always count your chain stitches on the front. You start and add to your foundation row on the front or right side of the chain.

Crochet instructions always tell you how many chains to make and where to start your work on the foundation chain.

Count chains from the front of the chain. Begin counting with the first complete stitch above the slip knot.

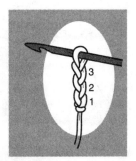

The chain's back has small bumpy loops.

Pointers

Counting chains means the same thing as *counting chain stitches.* For example, if you see the instruction "count 20 chains," you do not have to make 20 individual foundation chains. Instead, you make one foundation chain of 20 stitches.

Turning Chains

Obviously, at some point you have to quit making your foundation chain and actually add rows above it. To prepare to begin a new row, you make *turning chains*.

When you come to the end of a row, you need to work a certain number of chain stitches to bring your work to the height of the next row. This height is determined by the kind of stitch you will be using on that row: The taller the stitch, the greater the number of extra chains you'll have to make.

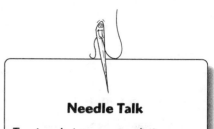

Needle Talk

Turning chains are extra chain stitches you make at the end of each row to accommodate for the height of the stitch of the next row.

Different stitches are different heights, and turning chains enable you accommodate for the stitch height.

The following chart shows the number of turning chains needed to accommodate for different crochet stitches. Granted, you haven't yet learned most of these stitches. Just bear with me; you'll need this information very soon!

Stitch Name	Turn Chains Needed
Slip stitch	1
Single crochet	1
Half-double crochet	2
Double crochet	3
Triple crochet	4

Using the information on this chart, suppose you are making a foundation row of 20 stitches and will

Snarls

If you forget to make turning chains at the end of a row, you will find yourself in a real pickle. The ends of your work will squash down because there won't be room for the row of stitches. To fix the problem, carefully unravel your work back to the end of the proceeding row and make the turning chains.

Yarn Spinning

Colorado State University's Gustafson Gallery contains two fabric books, the linen pages of which hold crochet samples dating back to the early 1900s. Each book holds more than 100 samples of beautiful stitchery, attesting to their makers' skill and need to document the work. These stitching books and others like them have been the basis for preserving some long-forgotten crochet techniques.

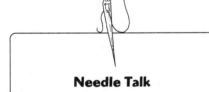

Needle Talk

A *slip stitch* is much like a chain stitch except that you are creating the stitch by working it from a foundation chain or other stitches. The slip stitch is abbreviated in instructions as *sl st.*

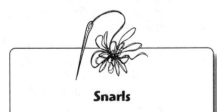

Snarls

Don't even try to work another stitch into a slip stitch. It is almost impossible to insert a hook into this stitch.

be double crocheting the next row. You would then need to chain 23 stitches:

> 20 stitches (foundation row) + 3 stitches (turning chains to accommodate for double crochet) = 23 stitches

Whew. So much homework! But now you are ready to begin the basic stitches. Most fancy crocheting, as you'll learn in Chapter 22, is a variation of these stitches.

Basic Stitches

The stitches in this section are the basis for almost every crochet technique—no matter how fancy. As you follow along, why not make an example of every stitch you learn? You'll want to refer back to these samples later.

If you plan to make samples, use the same weight yarn and the same hook for each. I suggest a size G hook and worsted weight yarn because both are a nice medium size—not too small as to be hard to handle, and not so large as to be cumbersome.

Slip Stitch (sl st)

The slip stitch is the smallest of all the crochet stitches. It is used mainly for joining (such as a ring or seams) and moving across existing stitches without obscuring them. It's also an ideal stitch to use as a finish because it makes a nice firm edge.

Making a slip stitch is easy. The only difference between making a slip stitch and a chain stitch is that you are now working off a foundation chain or off other stitches. Because you already know how to do a chain stitch, you know how to make a slip stitch.

To make a slip stitch, insert your hook, front to back, under the two top loops of a chain or stitch. Yarn over, and in one motion pull through the chain or stitch and the loop on your hook. One loop remains on the hook.

Many circular items such as doilies and tablecloths begin with the foundation chain joined in a ring. The slip stitch is what is used to join the ring.

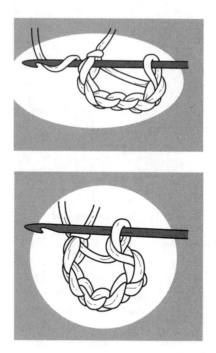

To use a slip stitch to join a ring, insert your hook under the two top loops of the first foundation chain, and then yarn over.

Pull the hook through the chain and the loop on the hook. One loop remains on the hook, and you have now completed a slip stitch and made a ring.

As we explore patterns and finishing, we'll come back to the slip stitch.

Single Crochet (sc)

Single crochet is truly the "basic" of all the crochet stitches. You will use it over and over when you start to make projects.

To make single crochet stitch, begin with a foundation chain. Make sure that the front side of the chain is facing you, then follow these steps.

Count to the second chain from the hook. Insert the hook, front to back, under the two top loops of the foundation chain.

You now have two loops on your hook: the original loop, and the "loop" made from the two strands of yarn you went under. Yarn over, pulling through the "loop" of two strands.

You again have two loops on your hook.

Yarn over again and pull through both loops on your hook. You now have one loop left on your needle and have just made your first single crochet!

If you're following along making a sample, go ahead and finish out your row in single crochet. When you get to the end of the foundation chain, make 1 turn chain to accommodate the height of the single crochet. Now, with the hook in your work, turn your work so that the reverse side is facing you.

The second row in single crochet might seem different from the first because you will be working into the first row's single crochet stitches rather than into a foundation chain. Actually, the procedure is exactly the same: You insert the crochet hook, front to back, into the two loops at the top of the crocheted stitch; then you complete the stitch.

Continue practicing your single crochet stitches until you feel comfortable with the concept.

Needle Talk

Single crochet is the most basic of crochet stitches and is abbreviated *sc*. To complete a single crochet stitch, insert the hook through a chain (or stitch); yarn over; pull the loop through the chain (or stitch); yarn over again; and pull through both loops on the hook.

Half-Double Crochet (hdc)

The half-double crochet stitch is slightly taller than the single crochet. The single crochet requires 1 turning chain; the half-double requires 2 turning chains. This stitch is the first of the basic stitches that requires a yarn over *before* you insert the hook.

To make a half-double crochet stitch, begin with a foundation chain. With the front side of the foundation chain facing you, yarn over the hook.

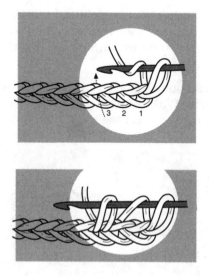

Insert the hook, front to back, under the 2 top loops of the third chain from the hook. Yarn over and pull the yarn through to draw up a loop.

There are now 3 loops on your hook. Yarn over and pull through all 3 loops.

Congratulations. You have now completed a half-double crochet stitch.

If you're following along making a sample, go ahead and finish out your row in half-double crochet. When you get to the end of the foundation chain, make 2 turn chains to accommodate the height of the half-double crochet. Now, with the hook in your work, turn your work so that the reverse side is facing you.

Continue practicing your half-double crochet stitches until you feel comfortable with the concept.

Needle Talk

Half-double crochet is a cross between a single crochet stitch and a double crochet stitch and is abbreviated *hdc*. To complete a half-double crochet stitch, begin with a yarn over; insert the hook into a stitch; pull through the stitch; do another yarn over; and pull through the three loops on your hook.

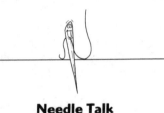

Needle Talk

Double crochet is a versatile stitch and is abbreviated *dc*. To make the double crochet stitch, begin with a yarn over; then insert the hook into a stitch; pull through the loop; yarn over and pull through 2 loops; yarn over and pull through the remaining loops.

Double Crochet (dc)

Double crochet is one of the most called-for stitches in patterns. As with the half-double crochet stitch, you start with a yarn over before you insert the hook. Because the double crochet has one more yarn over than does the half-double crochet, it's taller than the half-double crochet stitch.

Double crochet has one significant difference over the stitches you've already learned. When you begin a row, you need to count the turning chain as the first double crochet stitch.

To make a double crochet stitch, begin with a foundation chain. With the front side of the foundation chain facing you, yarn over the hook, then follow these steps:

Insert the hook, front to back, under the top 2 loops of the fourth chain from the hook.

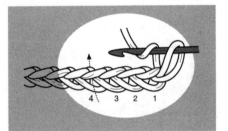

Pull through the loop. You have 3 loops on your hook. Yarn over again.

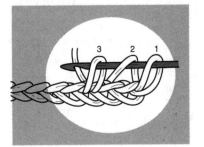

Pull through the 2 loops closest to the hook's point. Two loops remain on the hook.

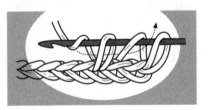

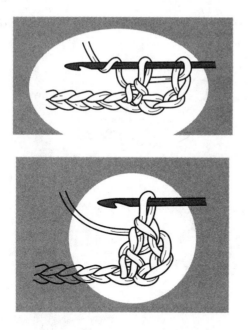

Yarn over once more, and pull through the 2 remaining loops.

You now have a single loop remaining on the hook.

Nice work. You just completed a double crochet stitch.

If you're following along making a sample, go ahead and finish out your row in double crochet. Remember that you'll actually complete one fewer double crochet than the row contains stitches because the turn chains count as the first double crochet.

When you get to the end of the foundation chain, make 3 turn chains to accommodate the height of the double crochet. Now, with the hook in your work, turn your work so that the reverse side is facing you.

Continue practicing your double crochet stitches as long as you like.

Snarls

It is important to count double crochet stitches consistently and correctly. Remember that the 3 turning stitches you make at the end of your previous row count as the first double-crochet stitch of the next row.

Triple Crochet (trc)

Triple crochet, the last of the basic stitches, is also the tallest. This stitch starts with 2 yarn overs before you insert the hook. Working this stitch is similar to working double crochet; you just need to work one more yarn over. Also, double crochet equals 3 turn chains, while triple crochet equals 4. As with double crochet, the first chain or turning chain counts as the first stitch.

171

To make a triple crochet stitch, begin with a foundation chain. With the front side of the foundation chain facing you, yarn over the hook twice then follow these steps:

Insert the hook, front to back, under the top 2 loops of the fifth chain from the hook. Pull through the loop. You now have 4 loops on the hook.

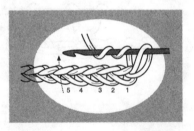

Yarn over and pull through the first 2 loops closest to the point of the hook; then yarn over again and pull through the next 2 loops closest to the point of the hook.

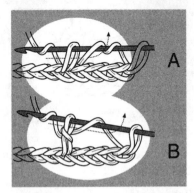

Two loops remain on the hook. Yarn over one last time and pull through both loops.

One loop remains on your hook.

Excellent. You've just made a triple crochet stitch.

If you're following along, making a sample, go ahead and finish out your row in triple crochet. Remember that you'll actually complete one fewer triple crochet than the row contains stitches because the turn chains count as the first triple crochet.

When you get to the end of the foundation chain, make 4 turn chains to accommodate the height of the triple crochet. Now, with the hook in your work, turn your work so that the reverse side is facing you.

Continue practicing your triple crochet stitches as long as you like.

> **Needle Talk**
>
> A *triple-crochet stitch* is abbreviated *trc*. To make this stitch, yarn over the hook twice; insert the hook into a stitch; yarn over again and pull through the first 2 loops (the 2 closest to the point); yarn over again and pull through the next 2 loops; yarn over one last time and pull through the remaining 2 loops.

Left-Handed Crochet

Can lefties crochet? Absolutely! You just need to adjust some of the basic directions in this chapter.

Before you begin this section, read the instructions and tips at the beginning of the chapter ("Basic Training"). All the information in that section is identical whether you're crocheting with your right or left hand.

The following sections illustrate a couple techniques specifically for left-handers: how to hold the yarn, how to make a chain stitch, and how to single crochet.

Left-Handed Basics

The beginning procedures in crochet, such as how to hold the hook and yarn, are the same for left-handed people as they are for right-handed people. Of course, you'll be doing the major work with your left, rather than right, hand. So, get out your hook and yarn, get comfortable, and let's begin.

The first thing you need to know is how to hold your hook. It's very simple; you have been doing it ever since you first held a pencil.

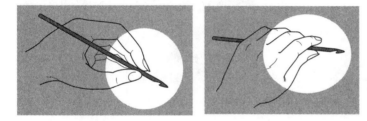

You hold the hook one of two ways. Either position and lightly grip your hook in your hand as you would hold a pencil, or hold the hook as you would grip a spoon when stirring something thick.

The choice is up to you. Use whichever way feels the most comfortable when you start to work.

Next, you need to get the yarn onto the hook. The instructions for making a slip knot don't differ whether you're right- or left-handed. Refer to the section "Slip Knot in the Making," earlier in this chapter, for directions on how to make a slip knot.

This is it! You have the slip knot on your hook and now you're ready to get down to the business of holding your yarn. Follow these steps:

With your right palm facing up, approximately 4 inches or so from your hook, grasp the yarn between your third and little fingers.

Draw the yarn toward you; thread the yarn over your middle finger, leading under your index finger.

Adjust the yarn so that it lies firmly but not tightly around your fingers.

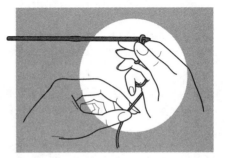

Initially, this configuration may feel a little strange. Practice holding a hook and yarn; soon this will become second nature.

Get Ready to Make Your First Chain

As you have already read in this chapter, the foundation chain is the base of all crochet. The following illustrations show you how to make a chain.

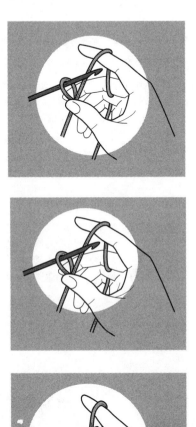

With yarn in hand and on the hook, use your thumb and middle finger to grab the slip knot right below the hook.

Now use the crochet hook to catch the yarn between your thumb and finger.

Pull the loop through the first loop on your hook.

Congratulations! You have completed your first chain stitch.

Make another chain, and another. When the row of chains gets too long, pull back on your yarn (down to the first loop) and start again.

Snarls

Because this section only details those concepts that are different for south-paws, you could get very confused reading only the left-handed information and skipping over the material at the beginning of the chapter. If you haven't done so yet, go back and read the basic informa-tion at the start of the chapter.

If you haven't already, review the section "The Base of All Crochet: the Foundation Chain" earlier in this chapter. It's important as you read the next section that you can recognize the front and back of the foundation chain.

Left-Handed Single Crochet (sc)

You've reached a moment of truth. Get ready to crochet!

To try out the single crochet, I suggest a size G needle and worsted-weight yarn; both are a good medium weight with which to start practicing.

To make single crochet stitch, begin with a foundation chain. Make sure that the front side of the chain is facing you, then follow these steps:

Count to the second chain from the hook. Insert the hook, front to back, under the top 2 loops of the foundation chain.

Yarn over and pull the loop through the founda-tion chain.

You now have 2 loops on your hook, yarn over again and pull through both loops on the hook. One loop remains.

Kudos to you! You just completed your first single crochet stitch.

If you're following along making a sample, go ahead and finish out your row in single crochet. When you get to the end of the foundation chain, make 1 turn chain to accommodate the height of the single crochet. Now, with the hook in your work, turn your work so that the reverse side is facing you.

The second row in single crochet might seem different from the first because you will be working into the first row's single crochet stitches. Actually, the procedure is exactly the same: You insert the crochet hook, front to back, into the 2 loops at the top of the crocheted stitch, and then finish the stitch.

Continue practicing your single crochet stitches. Pretty soon it will start to feel natural.

Other Basic Stitches

There are three additional basic crochet stitches: half-double, double, and triple crochet. Knowing how to do a single crochet stitch gives you the skills necessary to do all these other stitches on your own.

Refer once again to the beginning of this chapter to see how each stitch is formed. Also, double check on how many yarn overs are needed to work each stitch, and how many turn chains are necessary to make before you can start another row.

Pointers

If you need additional clarification on each of the remaining stitches, hold a mirror next to the illustration. You will see the image reversed, showing the way you would be working it with your left hand.

The Least You Need to Know

➤ Your way is the right way. Hold your hook and yarn so that it's comfortable for you.

➤ Foundation chains are the basis on which you build your crochet fabric.

➤ A yarn over (yo) is the most basic of all crochet fundamentals.

➤ Each stitch is abbreviated a specific way; once you know those abbreviations, you can read crochet patterns.

➤ Left-handed crochet is a mirror of right-handed crochet.

Chapter 18

Crochet a Cozy Afghan

In This Chapter

➤ The supplies you'll need to get started

➤ How to crochet an impressive afghan in almost no time

➤ Additional variations and ideas with your basic pattern

Afghans. Where would crocheting be without them?

Back in the 70s, my grandma gave me a swanky ripple afghan comprised of orange, yellow, and green stripes. Perhaps the color scheme wasn't timeless, but this gem is still a staple in my house and a constant companion come cool weather. Afghans are not only incredibly functional; they're also a lot of fun to make.

Sadly, because some truly atrocious afghans have been designed and crocheted over the years, they've gotten a bad rap. The pattern in this chapter should put the scoffers out of business.

This project has a lot to recommend it: It's fast, made relatively inexpensively, looks great, offers multiple color-combination possibilities, and is as thick as the dickens. In addition, as with all the patterns in this book, you can dink with the basic structure and look and never make the same afghan twice.

Cold winter winds are blowing outside, so let's get crackin'!

What Do I Need?

As with most projects in this guide, gauge matters very little. You're going to end up with a gauge of about 4 stitches per 3 inches, but a little variation one way or another won't matter.

To make an afghan that's about 60 inches long (plus fringe) by 40 inches wide, you'll need these supplies:

➤ About 72 ounces (about 4,700 yards) of worsted-weight yarn. Because of the heft of this afghan, acrylic is really your best bet; it'll machine wash and dry easily and emerge softer and fluffier than ever. If you buy 4-ounce acrylic skeins, you'll need 18 skeins. You crochet this afghan by combining three different strands of yarn into one strand, so you might want to choose 9 skeins in one color and 9 in another; or you might want to choose 6 skeins in three different colors. Or you might want to choose all the skeins in one color. The color combination is entirely up to you.

Pointers

Acrylic yarn often doesn't have a dye lot. (For a refresher on dye lot, see Chapter 2.) Generally, if this is the case, a banner will run across the bottom of the front label touting, "No dye lot."

➤ A size Q crochet hook. This size is enormous, halfway resembling a garden spade. You can find this size hook at craft or super-department stores (such as Wal-Mart or Meijer). You'll not only use the hook to crochet the afghan; when you finish, you'll also use it to attach fringe around two of the edges. And in an emergency, it makes a great backscratcher.

➤ A yarn needle for weaving in the yarn ends.

➤ A yardstick, ruler, or other straight surface for measuring the fringe.

How Do I Make It?

If you want to crochet something quickly, you use big needles and thick yarn. Worsted weight isn't so thick on its own, however, so we need a way to fatten it up. Consequently, you're going to triple its thickness by crocheting using three strands at a time.

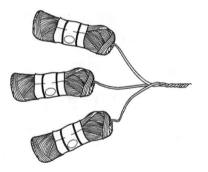

You combine three strands of yarn into one to make this chunky afghan.

With the 3 strands of yarn together, start by making a chain of 76 stitches.

Turn.

First row: In second chain from needle, single crochet. Single crochet across the row. At end of the row, make 1 turn chain and turn.

Remaining rows: Repeat the first row a total of 70 times, or until afghan is as long as you want. Secure the last loop.

If you complete 70 rows, you'll have an afghan that is approximately 60" long and 40" high.

Guess what? You're finished with the crocheting! You're not, however, completely finished with the afghan.

Now use the yarn needle to weave in all the ends.

Next, you're going to add fringe to the two shorter sides of the afghan.

Here's how to add fringe:

1. Cut pieces of yarn that are about 12" long. This makes about $5\frac{1}{2}$" fringe. If you want longer or shorter fringe, cut a different size. You'll need about 150 pieces of cut yarn, give or take about 20. I'd cut 150 pieces, and then cut more on an as-needed basis as you're finishing up the fringe.

2. Take 4 strands of the cut yarn in your hand, and line them up (to even out the ends).

3. Fold the 4 strands in half.

Yarn Spinning

One Christmas several years ago I made my sister an afghan similar to the one in this chapter. She loved it, but her two kids loved it more, rarely letting her use it. Consequently, the next Christmas I made one for each of the kids. But the dog got territorial about the afghans and took permanent ownership. So—you guessed it—with some embarrassment, I made the dog an afghan.

4. Using the crochet hook, insert the hook from the top to the bottom of the afghan. Grab the folded yarn with the crochet hook and pull it partway through the afghan.

5. Pull the ends of the fringe through the loop.

6. Continue adding fringe at intervals of about every two inches—more frequently if you want a fringier afghan.

7. Lay the afghan out on the floor and "comb" the fringe straight with your fingers. Using a pair of scissors, even up straggly ends.

Fringe finishes the afghan.

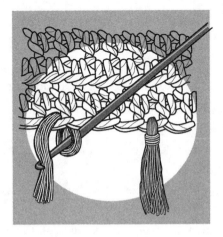

Pointers

Here's how this pattern would look abbreviated. Soon you'll be able to read patterns like this:

Ch 77. Turn. Sc in 2nd st from needle. Continue for 70 rows. Attach fringe at 2" intervals on short ends.

Variations on a Theme

The beauty of this afghan is that, although it's easy, it's also infinitely flexible. Try some of these other options:

➤ For a lacier look, crochet with only two strands of yarn rather than three. Your gauge is nearly the same, but the stitches are a bit lighter.

➤ Try mixing two colors on the afghan: Two strands of one color and one strand of the other. Then make the fringe solely out of the second color.

Pointers

Lion Brand makes a wonderful wool-blend yarn called Wool-Ease. Comprised of 80 percent acrylic and 20 percent wool, the yarn has the depth of wool and the easy care of acrylic. To receive a Lion Brand catalog, call 1–800–258-YARN (9276).

➤ If you're ready for a challenge, work stripes on the afghan: about 10 rows of each color. You can then make the fringe coordinate with the stripes.

➤ Make an afghan in the colors of your favorite sports-lover's favorite team. This would be a pretty kickin' piece in, say, classic Brooklyn Dodgers white and blue.

➤ Fashion a memorable baby shower gift by making this afghan using two strands of baby-weight yarn and a size H crochet hook.

The Least You Need to Know

➤ By doubling or tripling yarn and using a large crochet hook, you can finish a large project in a relatively short amount of time.

➤ Acrylic yarn often is the best choice when making heavy pieces that would be difficult to care for if they couldn't be machine washed and dried.

➤ Use a crochet hook to attach fringe.

➤ The afghan in this chapter is adaptable to any color combination, yarn texture, or size.

Chapter 19

Shaping Your Work

In This Chapter

➤ Adding and subtracting stitches

➤ Big changes happen depending on the way you insert your hook

➤ Working with circles and squares

➤ The Granny Square makes a cameo

You've learned a lot already. You know how to make a foundation chain, as well as how to single, half-double, double, and triple crochet. Amazing! And you've tested your skills on a fun cozy afghan.

Now you're ready to learn some more advanced crochet techniques. In this chapter, you'll learn to add and subtract stitches (called increasing and decreasing). As a bonus, you'll learn to break a few rules while stitching, playing with where you insert the hook and gallantly crocheting around in circles, rather than back and forth in rows.

Are you intrigued? Then read on.

Common Shaping Abbreviations

The following abbreviations are commonly used to indicate shaping in crochet. For a full list of knit and crochet abbreviations, see the tearcard at the front of this book.

Abbreviation...	What It Means...
1 sc dec	Single-crochet decrease
inc	Increase
dec 1 dc	Double-crochet decrease
fpdc	Front post double crochet
bpdc	Back post double crochet

The following sections explain these funky-looking abbreviations.

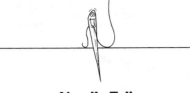

Upping the Ante

All is not even in crochet. A little increasing adds interest. To increase, no matter what the stitch, you work two stitches in the same spot.

To try increasing, begin with a foundation chain. Make sure that the front side of the chain is facing you. Work one or more rows of single crochet, chain 1 and turn.

At the beginning of the next row, increase one single crochet by working 2 single crochets into the first stitch. At the end of the row also work an increase. You now have 2 more single crochets on the row than you started with.

Increasing two stitches: one at the beginning and one at the end of the row.

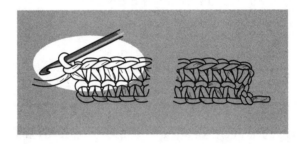

Less Is More—Sometimes

The buddy of increasing stitches is—you guessed it—decreasing stitches. Like increasing, decreasing enables you to shape the look of what you're crocheting.

To complete a decrease, you have to start with two partially worked stitches. Sound complicated? It's not.

Singles, Anyone? Decreasing in Single Crochet

To decrease in single crochet, you partially complete 2 stitches, and then merge them together. Here's how:

At the place where you want to decrease, insert the hook into the top two loops of the next stitch, yarn over, and pull through a loop. Don't finish the stitch!

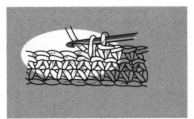

Insert the hook into the next stitch, yarn over, and pull through a loop. You now have 3 loops on your hook.

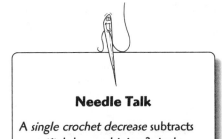

Yarn over one more time. This time, pull through all 3 loops on your hook.

You've just decreased a stitch on a single crochet row!

If you're actually following along making a swatch, continue practicing your decreases. Don't worry about your swatch becoming misshapen; you're learning a valuable new skill.

Decreasing in Double Crochet

Decreasing in double crochet is very much like decreasing in single crochet. Here's all you need to do:

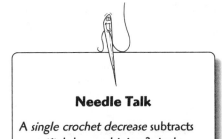

Needle Talk

A *single crochet decrease* subtracts one stitch by combining 2 single crochets. It is abbreviated *1 sc dec.*

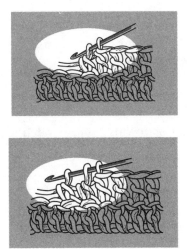

At the place where you want to decrease, work a double crochet down to 2 loops on your hook.

Yarn over, insert the hook into the top 2 loops of the next stitch, and work that stitch down until you have 3 loops on the hook.

187

Yarn over 1 more time and pull through all 3 loops.

You have just completed your first decrease in double crochet.

Decrease in Triple Crochet

You work a triple crochet decrease the same way you work the double crochet decrease. The only difference is that you begin each triple crochet with 2 yarn overs; consequently, you have to complete one more step to get down to 2 loops.

As with a double crochet decrease, when you have 3 loops on the hook, work a final yarn over and pull the yarn through all 3 loops.

Needle Talk

A *double crochet decrease* subtracts one stitch by combining two double crochets. It is abbreviated *dec 1 dc.*

New Threads

Up to this point, you've worked back and forth, turning your crochet when you hit the end of a row. Now it's time to break a few rules and give your work a different look. Slight changes in how you crochet can have a huge impact on the look of your pieces.

Working Under One Loop

Every sample you've done so far has had you inserting your hook under the 2 top loops of a stitch. Often, however, crochet instructions direct you to insert your hook under only 1 loop of a stitch. You can then insert the hook under the back loop only or under the front loop only. Each of these procedures forms a ridge that gives your finished fabric a different appearance from inserting under both loops.

To try inserting the hook into only 1 loop, start with a small swatch of single crochet.

Working across the row and inserting the hook into the back loop only makes a front ridge all the way across the row. If you're working along on a swatch, turn your work and crochet another row working in the back loops only.

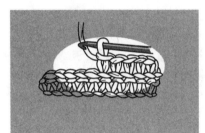

Insert your hook in the back loop only.

Pointers

When you work in the back loop only of a stitch, you form a ridge on the front of your work. When you work in the front loop only, you form a ridge on the back of your work.

You can use the same concept to insert your hook into the front loop only of each stitch, which causes a ridge to appear on the back.

Working Around the Post of a Stitch

Another interesting technique also involves how you insert the hook. You have gone from working under two loops to working only under one loop. Now you won't work through *any* loops.

Instead, you'll work using a stitch in the row below. This is called *working around the post of a stitch*. This procedure works best with double crochet or triple crochet stitches.

You can work around the post of a previous stitch in one of two ways: around the front of a post or around the back of a post.

If you want to try this new stitch, make a small swatch of about 20 stitches of double crochet.

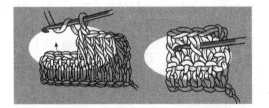

To work a front post double crochet, yarn over. Then insert the hook by going behind *the post of the stitch in the row below.*

189

Complete the double crochet as you normally would.

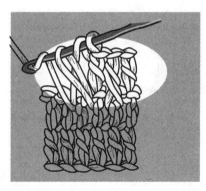

The front-post double crochet stitch is three-dimensional. If you're working on a swatch, work across the row by alternating one stitch of regular double crochet with one stitch of front-post double crochet. You'll see the difference in these stitches.

The back-post double crochet stitch is similar to the front-post double crochet. The only difference is that you're inserting your hook into the back of the post of the row below.

If you want to try this new stitch, make a small swatch of about 20 stitches of double crochet.

If you're working on a swatch, work across the row by alternating one stitch of regular double crochet with one stitch of back-post double crochet.

Needle Talk

A *front-post double crochet* is a special stitch that involves working into the front of the post of a crochet stitch on the row below. It is abbreviated *fpdc*.

To work a back post double crochet, yarn over. Then insert the hook by going in front of *the post of the stitch in the row below.*

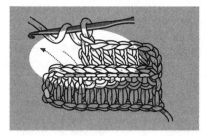

Complete the double crochet as you normally would.

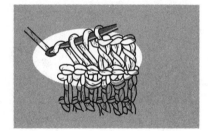

Pointers

To create the look of knitted ribbing, work two front-post double crochets stitches followed by 2 regular double crochets. Continue to alternate these stitches.

Crocheting Around in Circles and Squares

All is not straight in crochet. Working in circles and squares (called *motifs*) is one of the most interesting concepts you can learn.

You can make an endless number of projects—from home decor to fashion—by working squares and circles around a central point. To create this "central point," you use a slip stitch to join a small chain; the result is a ring.

How to Work Around and Around

To begin working around rather than back and forth, follow these steps:

1. Make a foundation chain of about 4 stitches. This number might vary slightly based on the project you're making, but 4 stitches is a good average.

2. With the right side of the chain facing you, insert your hook into the first chain, going under the 2 top loops. You're going to slip stitch the 2 ends of the loop together.

3. Yarn over the hook, draw through both the first chain and the loop on your hook. You've just completed the closing slip stitch.

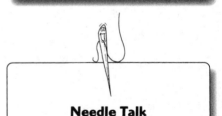

Needle Talk

A *back-post double crochet* is a special stitch that involves working into the back of the post of a crochet stitch on the row. It is abbreviated as *bpdc*.

Needle Talk

Motifs, in crochet, are pieces worked around a central point rather than back and forth. Doilies and Granny Squares are 2 examples of motifs.

Using slip stitch to turn a foundation chain into a ring.

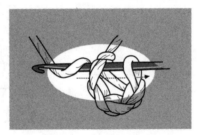

After you form the ring, you work stitches into the center *over* the chain loop. The stitches are worked as they would be on a flat foundation chain; the only difference is you'll be working in rounds.

Want to see this in action? Here's how to work single crochet stitches into the center ring:

1. Insert your crochet hook, front to back, into the center of the ring.

2. Work a single crochet stitch into the ring over the chain-loop.

3. Add seven more single crochet stitches into the ring, working around the ring as you go. The ring now holds a total of 8 single crochet stitches.

Making a single crochet in the ring.

4. Now close your round with a slip stitch. Insert the hook under the top 2 loops of the first single crochet stitch. Yarn over; draw through both loops on your hook. You have just completed Round 1.

When working in rounds, mark the last stitch in each round with a small safety pin. Move the pin up on each round so you will know when you have come to the end of that round.

Mark the beginning of rounds with a safety pin.

Move up the pin with each row.

Making the Circle Behave

As you might guess, if you keep the number of stitches in the round constant, you'll make more of a tube than a flat circle. With the second and all succeeding rounds, then, you must increase stitches steadily. Here is a helpful guide:

Round 1: Given number of stitches.

Round 2: Double given number of stitches.

Round 3: Increase one stitch in every other stitch.

Round 4: Increase one stitch in every third stitch.

Round 5: Increase one stitch in every fourth stitch.

Can you see a pattern? Continue this increase pattern on each succeeding round.

To work Round 2, then, increase 1 single crochet stitch in each of the previous stitches. If you started with 8 single crochet stitches, you will have 16 when you finish the round.

Working Rounds in Double and Triple Crochet

When you work in rounds with double or triple crochet stitches, you have to bring your work up to the height of the stitch you will be creating. To do so, make the number of chains equal to the height of the stitch. These chains always count as the first stitch on the round. Close the round after working your stitches by slip stitching in the top chain, going under the two top loops.

Grannies Have More Fun

The Granny Square is the most famous of all motifs. Who hasn't snuggled up under a Granny Square afghan? At the very least, we've all delighted in the variety of colors that can go on forever and be adapted to any home décor. And here's the best part: It's one of the easiest crochet projects you can undertake. So get ready to have some good old-fashioned granny fun.

As you learned, to make a circle motif you have to start with a ring. The difference between making a circle and a square motif is, of course, making corners. Sounds complex? Lucky you, it's not.

Here's how to make a fabulous Granny Square—the foundation for all types of creative projects. This Granny Square is made of double crochet stitches:

1. Make a center ring by making a foundation chain of 6 stitches and joining the stitches with a slip stitch.

2. Bring your work up to double crochet stitch height by chaining 3 stitches. These stitches are the first stitch of the next round.

3. Now work 2 double crochets in the ring by inserting your needle into the center of the chain space.

4. Chain 3 stitches; these stitches make up your first corner space.

5. Work 3 more double crochet stitches into the ring and chain 3 stitches for the next corner space.

6. Repeat step 5 two more times.

7. Close the square by slip stitching into the top of the first chain-3 you made at the beginning of the row.

Closing the first round of a Granny Square.

8. Slip stitch into the top of next two double crochet stitches; slip stitch into the corner space. Chain 3.

9. In the same corner space, make 2 double crochets; then chain 3 for a new corner.

10. Complete 3 double crochets in the same corner space. You just made the first corner of Round 2. Chain 1.

11. In the next corner space, work 3 double crochets, chain 3, and work 3 double crochets. You've now completed the next corner. Chain 1.

12. Continue in this manner for the next two corner spaces.

Working around the corners of a Granny Square.

13. To close the round, slip stitch on top of the first chain 3 as you did in Round 1. This completes Round 2. Round 3 starts out the same as Round 2.

14. Slip stitch into the top of next 2 double crochets; slip stitch into the corner space.

15. Chain 3; in the same corner space make 2 double crochets, chain 3 for a new corner, and make 3 double crochets all in the same space. This is the first corner of Round 3.

Completing the first corner of Round 3.

16. Chain 1. Skip the next 3 double crochets, and complete 3 double crochets in the next space from the previous row; this space appears between 2 clusters of double crochet stitches.

17. In the next corner, complete 3 double crochets, chain 3, and complete 3 double crochets.

18. Continue working corners, working double crochet stitches into spaces between corners, and using slip stitches to close up rounds.

Once you get the hang of Granny Squares, they're easy, aren't they? You can make them any size you want, use fine or bulky yarn, and change color between rows. (You'll learn all about changing color in the next chapter.)

Pointers

You might get so charged up about Granny Squares that you decide to tackle an afghan. If so, as you finish each square, stack that square on top of the other completed squares. Each square in the stack should be the same size as the others. Uniform square size is very important because when it comes time to put the squares together, if the squares aren't the same size and shape, you're going to end up with one funky afghan.

The Least You Need to Know

➤ Increasing is as easy as working 2 stitches in the same stitch.

➤ Decreasing is working 2 stitches together as one.

➤ How you insert your hook into a stitch before you work changes the look of the new stitch.

➤ Working circles or squares is simply a matter of working around rather than back and forth.

➤ The only difference between circles and squares is the addition of corners.

Chapter 20

Chameleon Moves: Becoming a Colorful Crocheter

In This Chapter

➤ Adding festive stripes

➤ Hiding in ends while you change colors

➤ Fun with bobbins

Up to this point you've worked in one color. There's no problem with monochromatic crocheting. Some of the most beautiful pieces—doilies, sweaters, scarves—are often made with only one color.

But what if you decide you're ready for a little more pizzazz? An extra challenge? A more eye-popping combination?

Changing crochet colors is as easy as changing your mind. With a few simple, basic steps you can change colors by working in stripes or color groups. If you're feeling particularly colorful today, read on.

Adding a New Color at the End of a Row

To get striping you need nothing more than a crochet hook, two colors of yarn, and your creativity. Here's how to stripe:

1. Make a foundation chain and work one row in single crochet. Work across the second row but stop right before the last stitch on the row.

2. Insert your hook into the stitch, yarn over, and pull up a loop. You have two loops on your hook.

*Preparing to change
colors.*

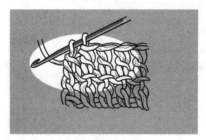

3. With the new yarn color, make a loop 4" long; using the hook, pull the loop through your stitch to close the single crochet. A single loop, of the second color, remains on your hook.

*Starting to crochet with
a second color.*

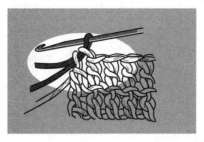

4. Work the neccesary number of turning chains and turn your work. You are now starting the row with your new color.

5. Trim the first color yarn, leaving about 4" from its end. You'll have to use a yarn needle to weave in these ends later. In the meantime, keep striping!

Pointers

When you run out of yarn while you are working, it's best—although not mandatory—to add another skein at the end of a row. Add the new skein the same way you just learned to add a new color.

Your Secret Mission: Hiding Ends in Color Blocks

To work in color blocks—changing colors in the middle of a row—you need to do a little planning ahead. Start the procedure about 3 stitches before where you want the actual color change to occur. By working this way, you can strategically—and almost magically—work the yarn end into your crocheting and save yourself some end-weaving time later.

Why don't you try making a swatch along with the instructions? Here's what you need to do:

1. Make a foundation chain of about 20 stitches and single crochet a couple rows.

2. In the third row, single crochet 8 stitches. You'll make a color change in the 11th stitch.

3. Prepare yourself for adding a second color by laying the new color on top of the second row of stitches.

> **Needle Talk**
>
> *Closing a stitch,* in crochet, refers to the step in which a stitch is finished and only one loop remains on the crochet hook. When changing colors, you always close the last stitch of the current color with the new color.

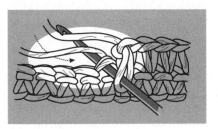

Placing the new color of yarn over the current color.

4. Work 2 single crochet stitches, simultaneously working over the yarn end that is laying on top of the stitches.

5. Now work 1 more single crochet stitch until you have 2 loops on the hook.

6. Pick up the second strand of yarn. With a yarn over, pull the new color through the two loops.

7. Close your stitch with the new color.

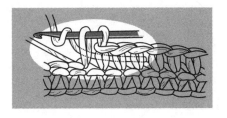

Closing the stitch with the new color.

8. Finish your swatch with the new color.

You just completed a color block. If you want to complete another color block, single crochet to 3 stitches before the stitch for which you want to change color, and follow these steps again.

Pointers

When you work in small color blocks of no more than 3 stitches, you do not have to cut your yarn. Instead, carry the yarn on top of the previous stitches and work over the new color. Then pick up the new color and close the stitch. Alternate colors across the row in this fashion.

Snarls

Be sure to run yarn loosely behind stitches when the yarn isn't in use. If the yarn is drawn up too tightly, the finished piece puckers.

Needle Talk

The *main color* is the predominant color in a multicolor piece; it is abbreviated *mc*. The *contrasting color(s)* is an accent color used in a piece; it is abbreviated *cc*. You may have more than one contrasting color.

Crocheting with Bobbins

Carrying yarn within stitches is clever, but if you carry more then one strand of yarn within your work, the fabric will become stiff and heavy. Does this mean you're restricted to using two colors only? Absolutely not. You can crochet with as many colors simultaneously as you want; you just have to work with small spools or bobbins. (For a description of bobbins, see Chapter 16.)

To use bobbins, you wind small amounts of colored yarn around each bobbin. You then crochet yarn from the bobbin as you need it. So long as you use a color every 5 or 6 stitches, you don't need to cut ends and weave them into the crocheted fabric. Instead, you can let yarn run across the back or wrong side of the piece, behind the stitches rather than worked into them.

Want to try an example? You'll need three yarns: a main color (mc), a second color (A), and a third color (B). Wind small amounts of A and B on separate bobbins; these bobbins will hang freely from the work—unobtrusive but ready for you when you need them.

1. Make a foundation row of 20 stitches.
2. With the main color, work two rows even in single crochet.

3. On the next row, work 2 single crochets with the main color, closing the second stitch with color A.

4. Work 2 single crochets with A, closing the second stitch with the main color.

5. Now work 2 single crochets, closing the second stitch with color B.

6. Repeat steps 3 through 5 one more time.

7. Repeat step 3 one more time.

You now have an intriguing, colorful row of three stitches. If you want to play longer with bobbins, try making this design; you've already worked the first three rows. To read the pattern, read odd rows left to right and even rows right to left.

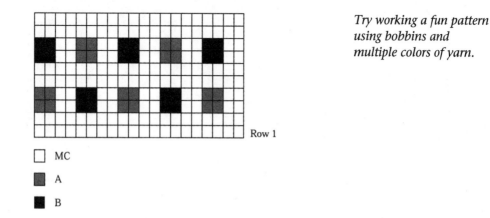

Row 1

Try working a fun pattern using bobbins and multiple colors of yarn.

☐ MC

■ A

■ B

The Least You Need to Know

➤ To change colors, always close the current stitch with the new color.

➤ You can carry the ends of new stitches in your crocheting and save yourself having to weave them in later.

➤ Bobbins let you work with many different colors simultaneously.

Chapter 21

Cracking the Code: Reading Crochet Patterns

In This Chapter

➤ Deciphering common crochet abbreviations

➤ Understanding repeats

➤ Dealing with wordless patterns

➤ Determining which set of directions to follow

Let's say you've been following along in this crochet section, swatching away, learning new stitches and techniques, playing with color, and increasing and decreasing with wild abandon. You're so fired up, you head over to your local bookstore, pick up a book of crochet patterns, find an afghan you want to make, flip to the instructions and…think you might have stumbled onto some secret battle plans from the Civil War.

What is all this muck?

Because some crochet designs would require reams and reams of paper to write out fully, a universal shorthand was devised for documenting patterns.

In this chapter, you'll learn about common abbreviations, how to read a chart, and what all those asterisks mean.

Common Crochet Abbreviations

Most common crochet terms have a universal abbreviation. In almost every pattern you read, including many of the stitch patterns in Chapter 22, these abbreviations allow complex patterns to be written quickly and cleanly. As you'll find when you begin crocheting more frequently, this abbreviation system actually makes patterns less cumbersome to read and follow.

Abbreviation	Full Name
blk	Block
blo	Back loop only
cc	Contrasting color
ch st	Chain stitch
ch	Chain
cont	Continue(ing)
dc	Double crochet
dec	Decrease(ing)
hdc	Half double crochet
inc	Increase(ing)
lp(s)	Loop(s)
mc	Main color
oz	Ounces
pat(s)	Pattern(s)
pc st	Popcorn stitch
rem	Remaining
rep	Repeat
rnd(s)	Round(s)
rs	Right side
sc	Single crochet
sl st	Slip stitch
slip	Slip
sp(s)	Space(s)
trc	Triple crochet
tog	Together
tr	Triple
ws	Wrong side
yo	Yarn over

Is This an Asterisk Before Me?

When you first glance at a crochet pattern, you might think the publisher forgot to take out the writer's proof marks. With the asterisks, parentheses, and addition signs, it all looks like someone got the wrong manuscript to the printer.

It's hard to believe, but patterns are written with standardized terms. By the time you finish this section when you see parentheses () and an asterisk *, you'll know just what to do. The system *does* make sense. If you need help, refer to the list of crochet abbreviations.

Acing the Asterisks

Asterisks play a crucial role in crochet patterns. They indicate the start of a section that you will repeat.

When you see any of these asterisk combinations, it means *repeat from*:

*

**

***

In other words, You need to repeat the instructions following the *, **, or *** as many times as given. You would first work the information given once. Then you would repeat that information as many times as specified.

Here's an example:

*Sc in first st. Repeat from * 5 more times.

This pattern is telling you to single crochet in the next stitch, and then repeat this step (the step following the asterisk) five more times.

Practicing with Parentheses

Parentheses work in much the same way as asterisks. When you see this

( )

it means *work what is in the parentheses as many times as given*. Here's an example:

(sc, dc, sc) 3 times

This means that you should single crochet, double crochet, and single crochet a total of three times.

Primed for the Pluses

Plus signs indicate that you should repeat something between the plus signs. When you see

+ to +

it means *work the instructions between the plus signs and repeat as many times as specified.* Here's an example:

+sc, dc, sc in next st+. Repeat + to + 5 more times.

This means you would single crochet, double crochet, and single crochet into the next stitch, and then repeat this action five more times.

Pointers

Reading PatternSpeak becomes easier when you really start to work from a pattern. If you're initially confused about what the instructions are saying, write them out in longhand and work through them step by step. This method might take a little extra time, but it will help you get used to reading patterns. In addition, it might save you the time and heart-break of ripping out and re-doing your work.

The Sounds of Silence: Patterns Without Words

Have you ever thumbed through pattern booklets where all the instructions are given in symbols? These symbols actually look like the stitches they represent. In fact, when you see an entire pattern worked out in symbols, it really looks very much like the completed project.

Reading symbols is an acquired skill. In fact, writing and reading in symbols isn't really any faster than writing and reading in crochet shorthand; this method simply makes the information international without requiring a language translation.

The following is a list of the basic stitches you might run across in symbol patterns:

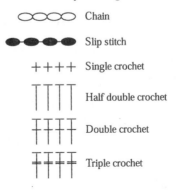

Chain

Slip stitch

Single crochet

Half double crochet

Double crochet

Triple crochet

Playing the Sizing Game

Often crochet patterns for clothing are written to fit differently sized people, and the patterns have to accommodate for the sizing differences. Variations in sizes are typically included in parentheses.

A pattern, for example, might begin like this:

To fit chest size 34" (36", 38", 40", 42")

This means that the entire pattern is written using this same parenthetical annotation for larger sizes. If you are making the 36" size, then, for any shaping or patterning instructions you will always follow the first number in the parentheses. For example, as you begin the pattern, you might see the following:

Ch 80 (90, 100, 110, 120)

Snarls

This parenthetical annotation system is wonderful for writing lots of instructions compactly, but it can be hazardous if you're not paying close attention. To avoid accidentally following the wrong sizing instructions, before you start your project, go through the pattern and circle the instructions for the size that you will be making. You then can easily see the numbers you need to follow.

If you were making the 36" size, you would make a foundation chain of 90—the first number in the parentheses. Follow this same system throughout the pattern.

The Least You Need to Know

➤ Universal abbreviations mean that patterns can be read and written more quickly and effectively.

➤ Asterisks, parentheses, and plus signs are used to indicate repeats in a pattern.

➤ Some patterns are written completely in symbols to make them universal without translation.

➤ If a pattern contains instructions for multiple sizes, go through and highlight all the instructions you'll be using for your size before you begin the project.

Chapter 22

Specialty Stitches and Patterns

In This Chapter

➤ Filet crochet, spaces, and blocks

➤ Afghan crochet holds more stitches than meet the eye

➤ Putting your stitch skills into patterns

➤ Crocheted motifs add depth and beauty to your work

No doubt when you first decided to learn to crochet, your interest was sparked by an exquisite, detailed design. "I want to do that!" you thought. You can. All of those intricate pieces were made with the basic skills and tools you've been reading about in the previous six chapters.

This chapter deals with some specialized crochet stitches and techniques; delicate and lacy filet crochet, functional and cuddly Afghan crochet, and a host of specialty stitches you can make by rearranging the basic stitches you've already learned.

This chapter uses a lot of the pattern-reading skills you learned in the previous chapter. If you get stuck reading some of these wacky symbols, flip back to Chapter 21 for help. Also, you might want to keep the tearcard from the front of the book handy for help with common crochet abbreviations.

We're Not Talking Fish Here

One of the most popular uses for crochet over the years has been *filet crochet*. Filet crochet is a unique art that creates images by filling in blocks over a background mesh of crochet.

Filet crochet is basic, fast, and enjoyable. Eager to learn how it's done? Let's start with the elements that make it up.

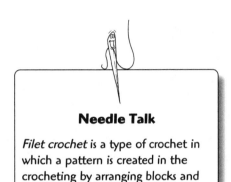

Filet in Spaces and Blocks—Oh, My!

Filet crochet is made up of two elements: background mesh and filled blocks.

Mesh can be put together in a number of different ways. Think of mesh as double or triple crochet stitches separated by chains to form little squares or spaces. These spaces are the background on which *blocks* of crochet are worked to form illustrations or patterns. You can work two spaces together as one, thus creating a double space. You can also work a lacet over a double space to form a lacier look.

The following table defines the different stitches and steps in filet crochet. You might want to refer to it as you work through the following sections.

Needle Talk

Filet crochet is a type of crochet in which a pattern is created in the crocheting by arranging blocks and spaces.

Filet Crochet Terms

Term	Definition
mesh	The filet background.
space	The element formed by chains separating double crochet stitches in the mesh.
double space	Two spaces worked as one.
block	A space filled in with double crochet stitches.
double block	Two spaces filled in with double crochet stitches.
lacet	Two chains, one single crochet and two chains worked over a double space.

Spinning the Web: Creating Your First Mesh Piece

Are you eager to make a sample of filet crochet? This section shows you how to create mesh by combining double crochet with chains. You can apply the concepts you learn in this section to any other filet crochet projects.

If you'll be following along, creating a swatch with the instructions, you'll need yarn and a crochet hook. A good medium-size combination is worsted weight yarn with a size H crochet hook, but you can use any yarn weight and hook size you choose.

Follow these steps to make your first mesh piece:

1. Make a foundation chain of 23 stitches.

Yarn Spinning

Over the years numerous subjects have been depicted in filet crochet—from simple botanicals to highly religious themes. During World War II, filet crochet contests awarded prizes to contestants who executed the most beautiful patriotic designs.

Pointers

Remember the symbols defined in Chapter 21? If not, here's a little reminder:

*, **, or *** means repeat as many times as given.

( ) means do what is in parentheses as many times as is given.

+ to + means repeat what is between these marks.

2. Work a double crochet in the eighth chain from the hook to make the first space. Do you know why you left the first 7 chains alone and double crocheted in the eighth chain from the hook? Look at this math:

   2 chains form the bottom of the first space

   3 chains count as the first double crochet on row 1 (the right side of the first space)

   2 chains form the top of the first space

   7 chains total

Double crochet in the eighth chain from the hook to create the first space.

3. To continue the row, follow this pattern:

   *Chain 2, skip the next 2 chains, double crochet in the next chain (1 space made), repeat from * 4 more times (total of 6 spaces have been made). Chain 5, turn.

   On the second row, the chain-5 will count as the first double crochet plus chain-2 space.

A row of spaces is made by working a double crochet, chain 2 pattern across the row.

4. Double crochet into the second double crochet on the row. You've now made a second space over the first space in the row.

5. To complete the row, follow this pattern:

   *Chain 2, 1 double crochet in next double crochet (space over space made), repeat from * 3 more times. Work last double crochet in fifth chain of initial chain-7 (final space made). Chain 5.

6. Repeat steps 4 and 5 for 4 more rows, working the last double crochet on each row in the third chain of turning chain-5.

   You now have completed 6 rows of mesh.

7. On the next row, work a beginning space over space, as you have done on the last 5 rows. Then make a double space as follows:

   Chain 5, skip the next double crochet, double crochet in the next double crochet.

   You've now made a double space: the chain-5 counts as 2 chains, 1 double crochet, and 2 chains.

8. Chain 5 again, work another double space. End the row by working a single space over the last space. Chain 5.

9. Start the next row by working a space over a space: double crochet into the second double crochet, as you have done on the other rows.

10. Now chain 2, skip 2 chains, double crochet into the next chain, chain 2, skip next 2 chains, and double crochet into next chain.

    You have now completed 2 spaces over a double space.

11. Repeat this procedure over the next double space. End the row working a space over a space.

Are you still with me? Do you like your swatch? It's very exciting to see how you can combine the basic steps you learned earlier—chaining and double crocheting—to create a new type of piece.

Filling in the Dots

To form a pattern on a mesh background, just create blocks of double crochet rather than spaces. In other words, rather than following this pattern to form a space:

> chain 2, 1 double crochet in next double crochet

You would follow this pattern:

> 3 double crochet

Filling in the blocks.

I told you this was easy!

Forming a Lacet

Up to this point, you've only worked single and double square blocks. You can also form a lacet, which has a lacier look, by following these steps:

1. At the end of the last double crochet, chain 3, skip the next 2 double crochets, single crochet into the next double crochet, chain 3, skip 2 double crochets, double crochet in the next double crochet.

213

Forming a lacet by single
crocheting rather than
double crocheting.

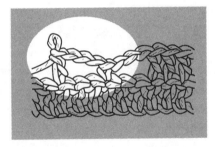

2. On the next row, work a double space over the lacet.

The row following a lacet.

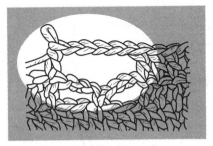

Increasing and Decreasing in Filet Crochet

When you increase and decrease in filet crochet, you can do so a block or space at a time. The pattern you're following always tells you when and how to increase or decrease, so after you have down the basic concepts, you're in fat city.

To increase a space and a block at the *beginning* of a row follow these two simple procedures:

To increase a block at the beginning of a row, chain 5 at the end of your last row. On the next row, double crochet into the fourth chain from the hook and each of the next 2 chains. Double crochet into the next double crochet. You've now made a block increase.

A simple block increase at
the beginning of a row.

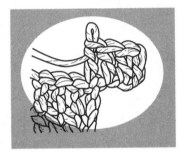

To increase a space at the beginning of a row, chain 5 at the end of your last row. On the next row, double crochet into the first double crochet. You've now made a space increase.

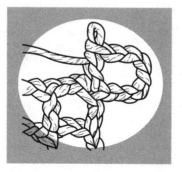

A simple space increase at the beginning of a row.

To increase a block at the *end* of a row, you have to follow a specific procedure. In essence, you are making a chain and a double crochet stitch at the same time. It sounds tricky, but it's really not so bad. Give it a try:

1. Work across the row to the last double crochet.

2. Working in the base of last double crochet, work another double crochet as follows: yarn over, pull through 1 loop (this step forms the base chain), complete the double crochet stitch.

3. When you have completed the stitch, repeat this process in the base of this stitch 2 more times. You have now completed a block increase.

A block increase at the beginning of a row.

To decrease in filet crochet, just leave your blocks and spaces unworked either at the beginning or end of a row. Let's take a look:

To decrease at the beginning of a row, slip stitch over the required double crochets or chains. Then chain the number required to complete the block or space.

Decreasing at the beginning of a row.

To decrease at the end of the row, stop working on the row at the point in which you want to decrease. Turn and start working on the next row.

Decreasing at the end of a row.

Reading a Filet Crochet Chart

Filet crochet patterns are written as charts. Often, a pattern begins with instructions in words, but after a certain point, refers you to the chart for the remaining instructions.

As you might expect, the dark areas indicate blocks and the white areas indicate spaces.

To read the chart, begin on row 1 and read from left to right. Read all odd-numbered rows from left to right and all even-numbered rows from right to left. If you are left-handed, read the odd-numbered rows from right to left and the even-numbered rows from left to right.

To find your place easily while you're reading the chart, you might affix a Post-It note under the row you're currently working on. You can then move up the Post-It note one row as you complete each row.

A filet crochet chart showing how to work the pattern.

Afghan (Tunisian) Crochet

When you hear "Afghan crochet," you might think of the item that is made: a cozy Granny Square number, for example. Actually, Afghan (Tunisian) crochet is a specific stitch that is very different from the stitches you have learned so far. It produces a thicker fabric, has a nice weight, and resembles knitting both in the execution and in the finished look.

Several things separate Afghan crochet from the other types of crochet you've learned so far. Afghan crochet requires a unique afghan hook (named after the stitch, of course). The hook is much longer than a regular crochet hook and resembles a mix between a single-pointed knitting needle and a crochet hook. This special hook is necessary because, unlike the crochet stitches you've learned so far, you keep all your stitches on the hook, just like you would in knitting. The final difference between Afghan crochet and traditional crochet is that you don't turn your work. Instead, you work two rows to make one row of stitches.

This section walks you through the procedure of Afghan crochet. If you want to follow along by creating your own swatch, I recommend that you use a straight rather than flexible hook. (To see the differences in these two hooks, turn back to Chapter 16.) The flexible afghan hook is a little harder to handle initially than is the straight hook, so it's best used after you have mastered the technique.

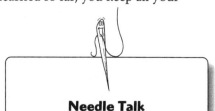

Needle Talk

Afghan (Tunisian) crochet is a special variation of crochet in which the stitches are held on the crochet hook. Special hooks are manufactured for this type of crochet.

217

Hooked on Afghans: Practice Makes Perfect

To start a piece in Afghan crochet, you begin with a foundation chain as you would in any other type of crochet. If you're swatching along with these instructions, cast on a foundation chain of about 20 chains. Now, here's where the magic begins:

1. In the second chain from the hook, insert the hook, front to back, under the 2 top loops.

2. Draw up a loop, leave the loop on your hook, and draw up another loop in the next chain (the third chain from the hook).

Drawing up loops to begin Afghan crochet.

3. Continue across the row, drawing up a loop in each chain, leaving them all on your hook.

Completing a row of loops.

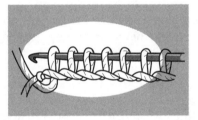

4. When you get to the end, count your loops. You should have the same number of loops as you had chains.

   Unlike the crochet techniques you've learned so far, the first loop on your hook counted as the first stitch.

5. Now you're going to complete the first row. Yarn over and draw through 1 loop.

Beginning to work back across the first row.

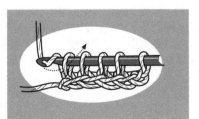

6. Yarn over and draw through 2 loops.

   You'll notice that the number of stitches on the hook is decreasing.

7. Work across the row as in step 6 until only 1 stitch remains on the hook. The last loop left on your hook always counts as your first stitch on the next row.

A completed row in Afghan crochet.

Now get ready for Row 2. This row also takes two procedures to complete:

1. Insert the hook horizontally through the front vertical bar (formed from the previous row) and draw up a loop.

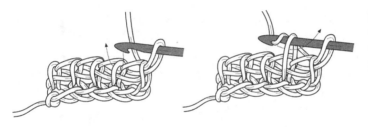

Beginning Row 2 by working through the vertical bars formed from the previous row.

2. Repeat this across in each vertical bar until you reach the last vertical bar.

3. Go through the last vertical bar to the back (through both vertical loops). These steps gives the piece a firm edge.

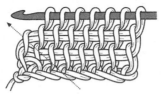

Finishing the first half of Row 2.

4. When you get to the end, count your loops. You should have the same number of loops as you had chains in your foundation chain.

5. The second half of this row is worked the same way as the second half of the first row. To complete this row, follow steps 5 through 7 in the previous section.

You repeat the second row (both halves) to form the pattern.

This nice sturdy stitch makes for cozy afghans and is also great for making some gorgeous outerwear, such as jackets and heavy scarves.

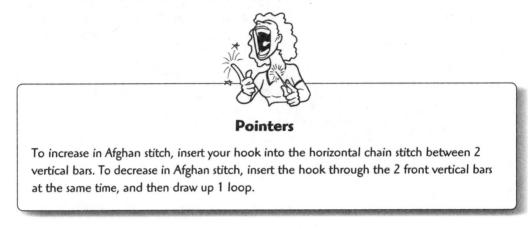

Pointers

To increase in Afghan stitch, insert your hook into the horizontal chain stitch between 2 vertical bars. To decrease in Afghan stitch, insert the hook through the 2 front vertical bars at the same time, and then draw up 1 loop.

A Stitch in Time

It's time to put all your knowledge to work and practice pattern stitches. The patterns that follow are representative of the kind you'll find in crochet instructions.

These patterns make heavy use of the pattern instructions and abbreviations you learned in Chapter 21. If you need help reading the instructions, refer back to that chapter.

Keeping It Simple

You've learned a lot, but you're not ready to rest on your laurels just yet—you're ready for more! This section contains several simple but attractive designs you can practice and integrate into your own crocheted designs.

The instructions that follow indicate the number of chains required and give you stitch multiples to make up the pattern.

Pointers

A *stitch multiple* is the number of stitches necessary to complete a pattern stitch. A pattern of dc, ch2, dc requires 4 stitches, so it would have a stitch multiple of 4. Often a stitch multiple includes an extra stitch or two at the beginning or end of a row of patterned stitches. For example, a stitch multiple of "4 plus 2" means you can start from a foundation chain of any number divisible by 4, plus an extra 2 stitches. For this example, you could use 14:

4 (stitch multiple) × 3 (number of times you want to repeat the stitch) + 2 = 14

This means you can work the pattern 3 times, plus have the extra 2 stitches required.

Start with the following three easy patterns.

Pattern 1.

Stitch multiple: Any length plus 1

Row 1: Sc in second ch from hook, and each ch across. Ch 1 turn.

Row 2: Working in front loop only, sc in first sc and each sc across.

Row 3: Sc in first sc, and each sc across.

Repeat **Rows 2** and **3** for pattern.

You can also do this pattern with a half-double and a double crochet stitch.

Pattern 2.

Stitch multiple: 2 plus 1

Row 1: Sc in 2nd ch from hook, *dc in next ch, sc in next ch; rep from * across. Ch 1 turn.

Row 2: Sc in first dc of row below, *dc in next sc of row below, sc in next dc of row below; rep from * across. Ch 1 turn. Repeat **Row 2** for pattern.

Pattern 3.

Stitch multiple: 2 plus 2

Row 1: Sc in 2nd ch from hook, *ch 1, skip 1 ch, sc in next ch; rep from * across. Ch 1 turn.

Row 2: *Sc in ch-1 space, ch 1; rep from * across, end with sc in top of turning ch. Ch 1 turn. Rep **Row 2** for pattern.

Cluster Stitches

Cluster stitches are groups of stitches that give the appearance of a single stitch. There are three distinct ways to form these stitches, even though the results appear quite similar.

Popcorn Stitch. Popcorn stitch is a group of completed stitches worked in the same place and then closed together with a slip stitch. In crochet patterns, popcorn stitch is abbreviated *pc st.*

To begin a popcorn stitch, make a foundation chain. If you want to follow along, make a foundation chain at least 20 chains long; then follow these steps:

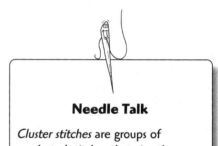

Needle Talk

Cluster stitches are groups of crocheted stitches that give the appearance of a single stitch.

In the eighth chain from the hook, work 5 double crochet stitches. When they are completed, slide the hook from the loop currently on it.

Insert the hook into the top of the first double crochet, going behind the stitches and pulling through the dropped loop.

To secure the popcorn stitch, chain 1.

Bobble Stitch. Bobble stitch differs from popcorn stitch in that it is made of double crochets that are not fully completed. These stitches are then closed to give the appearance of a single stitch.

To begin a bobble stitch, make a foundation chain. If you want to follow along, make a foundation chain at least 20 chains long; then follow these steps:

In the eighth chain from the hook, work a double crochet stitch until 1 loop remains on the hook. Repeat this same procedure 4 more times.

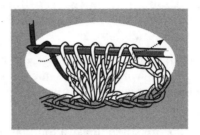

Yarn over and draw through all the loops on the hook.

Secure the bobble with a chain stitch.

Puff Stitch. Puff stitch is similar to a bobble stitch because it too is made up of incomplete stitches that are then closed to appear as a single stitch.

To begin a puff stitch, make a foundation chain. If you want to follow along, make a foundation chain at least 20 chains long; then follow these steps:

In the eighth chain from the hook, work a hdc, *yo, insert the hook, and pull up a loop. Repeat from * 2 more times. There are now 7 loops on the hook. Yo and draw through all the loops on the hook.

Close the puff stitch with a chain 1.

Shell and V-Stitches

Shell and V-stitches are also cluster stitches, but these multiples of stitches are worked into a single chain or stitch. Use at least a double crochet stitch to make these stitches; the effect of the shell is lost with short stitches such as single crochet or half-double crochet.

To begin, make a foundation chain. If you want to follow along, make a foundation chain at least 20 chains long.

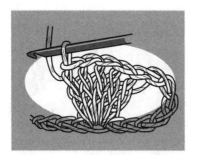

In the eighth chain from the hook, work 5 complete double crochets.

Pointers

To keep a shell stitch row even, skip as many chains or stitches as you have stitches on either side of your center stitch. If you are working two shell stitches next to each other, double the chains or stitches.

Variety Is the Spice of Crochet

Crochet is of course much more than just making "fabric." It's also about motifs. You've already been introduced to your first, the Granny Square. Let's go further back into crochet's past and work some of the most historically famous motifs.

Here, as you start, you might want to hum a few bars of "When Irish Eyes Are Smiling." Of all the wonderful, small motifs to crochet, none equals the romance of Irish Lace.

Irish Roses

Who hasn't seen wonderful examples of this incredible work, either in museums or as reproductions? Seemingly endless variations of Irish Crochet Rose motifs have been created and preserved over the years.

Instructions for Irish Crochet usually call for very fine thread. For ease in learning this technique, however, try your first Irish Rose using worsted-weight yarn and a size G crochet hook. You will be able to more easily see what to do. Now get ready to crochet a garden...

An eight-petal Irish Rose.

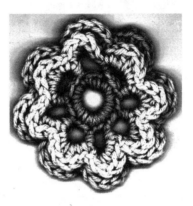

As with all motifs, begin by forming a center ring. Ch 8, join to form the ring.

Here's how to make an Irish rose:

> **Round 1:** Ch 1,12 sc in ring. Join in first sc. **Round 2:** Ch 5, *skip 1 sc, sc in next sc, ch 4, rep from * 5 more times, sl st in first ch of ch-5. **Round 3:** In each ch-loop, 1 sc, 1 hdc, 3 dc, 1 hdc, and 1 sc. **Round 4:** *Insert hook behind bar of next sc formed in Row 2, work 1 sc, ch 5, rep from * 5 more times. Join in first sc. **Round 5:** In each ch-loop, 1 sc, 1 hdc, 5 dc, 1 hdc, and 1 sc. **Round 6:** *Insert hook behind bar of next sc formed in Row 4, 1 sc, ch 6, rep from * 5 more times. Join in first sc. **Round 7:** In each ch-loop, 1 sc, 1 hdc, 7 dc, 1 hdc, 1 sc. Join behind bar of next sc in Round 6. Fasten off.

If you want to make a rose with more rounds, just continue adding in this same sequence.

Leaves for the Irish Rose

Every rose should be enhanced with a leaf or two. Here's how to make them:

Row 1: Ch 16, sc in 2nd ch from hook, and each ch across – 15 sc. Ch 3, working along bottom edge of foundation ch, sc in each ch across – 15 sc. Ch 3, working in back loops only from now on, sc in next 14 sc. Ch 3, turn. **Row 2:** Skip first sc, sc in each next 13 sc, 3 sc in ch-3 loop, sc in next 13 sc. Ch 3, turn. **Row 3:** Skip first sc, sc in each next 13 sc. Ch 3, skip 1 sc, sc in next 13 sc. Ch 3, turn. **Rows 4 & 5:** Rep Rows 2 & 3, working 12 sc. Fasten off.

You can increase the size of your leaf by continuing the established sequence.

A leaf to complete your Irish Rose.

The Least You Need to Know

➤ Filet crochet is as easy as putting blocks and spaces together.

➤ Afghan crochet breaks two rules: the tool you use and how you count stitches.

➤ Pattern stitches combine the basic crochet stitches in new ways.

➤ Shaped motifs add dimension to your work.

Chapter 23

Set a Stunning Table with Woven Placemats

In This Chapter

➤ The supplies you'll need to get started

➤ Instructions for stitching a plaid placemat that lets you practice filet crochet techniques

➤ Learning a little weaving and a new way to make fringe

➤ Additional ideas about yarn variations

One of the most exciting aspects of crochet is that the skill you learn for one type can be used for so many diverse projects. The simple single crochet stitch, for example, is one of the best stitches you can use to edge knit sweaters and afghans.

In this chapter, you'll use the procedure you learned to make filet crochet mesh and work it into an entirely different type project. You'll also get to practice a bit more with colorwork and learn to use a neat crochet bonus: simple weaving. The result is a unique plaid placemat that will look great in your house or make a welcome gift.

Let's get started!

What Do I Need?

The placemat is crocheted in two colors: a main color and a contrasting color. You can select two colors that are fairly close in tone, creating a subtle plaid, or two highly contrasting colors such as black and white.

To make a placemat that is approximately 20" wide and 14" tall, you'll need these supplies:

➤ Two different colors of worsted-weight yarn:

About 3 ounces (200 yards) of a main color (mc)

About 2 ounces (130 yards) of a contrasting color (cc)

Acrylic washes up well, but wool makes beautiful rustic placemats. Depending on how heavily these will be used, choose either a natural or synthetic fiber.

➤ A size H crochet hook.

➤ A ruler or yardstick.

➤ A yarn needle for weaving in the ends at the beginning and end of the project, and for weaving the contrasting horizontal threads through the placemat.

How Do I Make It?

This placemat looks much more complex than it is because you don't actually create the plaid look all at the same time. Instead, you first crochet the mat, creating stripes as you work. Then you weave stripes into the mat in the opposite direction of the crocheted stripes. The result is a very simple-to-execute plaid.

Gauge isn't so important in this pattern, but if you use a gauge counter, you'll find that one double crochet, one space, one double crochet, and one space make up about an inch.

Follow these steps to crochet the placemat:

1. Beginning with the main color, make a foundation chain of 55 stitches.

2. Double crochet in the fifth chain from the hook. Chain 1, double crochet in the second chain from the hook. Continue these two stitches all the way across a row.

Pointers

Does your first row look familiar? You are following the same pattern you used to create the filet crochet mesh in Chapter 22. Instead of filling in the blocks with double crochet stitches, however, you'll ultimately fill these mesh blocks by weaving yarn in the opposite direction from the direction you're crocheting.

3. At the end of the row, chain 4. Double crochet into the first double crochet on the preceding row.

4. Chain 1, double crochet into the next double crochet on the preceding row. Continue these two stitches across the entire row.

5. Follow steps 3 and 4 a total of 3 more times. Don't close the final stitch using the main color; you will be switching colors. You now have 5 rows of mesh in the main color.

6. Change to the contrasting color and work 2 rows of mesh.

7. Change back to the main color and work 5 more rows of mesh.

8. Follow steps 6 and 7 a total of 5 times. You now have crocheting 40 rows of mesh.

9. Pull through the final loop. Weave in all the yarn ends.

10. Now, use your ruler to cut lengths of yarn 60 inches long. Total, you'll need 20 lengths of the main color and 6 lengths of the contrasting color.

11. Thread the yarn needle with one of these lengths of the main color. Bring the needle to the very center of the yarn; you now have the needle threaded with a 30" double thickness of yarn.

12. Starting at one of the shorter sides of the placemat, insert the needle down through the first mesh hole, up through the next one, down through the next one, and so on all the way across the row. At the end of the row, snip the yarn where the needle is to free the needle.

    You have now woven the first length of yarn across the mat. Stretch the mat slightly, making sure that the yarn being woven in isn't puckering the fabric. Adjust the ends of yarn coming from both sides of the mat so that they're basically even; you'll be trimming these soon.

13. Thread the needle with a second length of the main color and weave this through, beginning by inserting the needle up, then down, then up, then down, all the way across the row.

Snarls

Be sure to weave in each strand of yarn in the opposite direction from the strand preceding it. If, for example, the strand preceding began with inserting the needle down through the hole, begin the next one by inserting the needle up through the hole.

Weave the yarn strands through the fabric to create the plaid look.

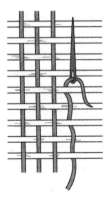

14. Continue weaving the yarn. Total, you will work the following:

    5 lengths of the main color
    2 lengths of the contrasting color
    5 lengths of the main color
    2 lengths of the contrasting color
    5 lengths of the main color
    2 lengths of the contrasting color
    5 lengths of the main color

15. Now, working across one side, gather 2 strands of yarn from the first length of yarn and 1 from the second, and tie these together into a slip knot. The knot should rest against the fabric of the placemat, with the ends hanging down to create the fringe.

Secure the yarn and create fringe by tying three strands together, in a slip knot, across opposite sides of the mat.

16. Follow step 15, tying the second strand of yarn from the second length with the 2 strands from the third.

17. Continue across the row, tying 3 strands together at a time.

18. Tie the fringe on the other side of the mat.

To finish: Trim the fringe ends to even them out.

Variations on a Theme

These placemats are a lot of fun to make; they're simple but look impressive when you're finished. Here are some additional thoughts about making your mats unique:

➤ Choose four bright colors and make a set of four placemats, alternating which color is the main color and which is the contrasting. The result will be a Fiestaware-type set in which the mats belong together but aren't completely homogenous.

➤ Make up a set of 4 placemats and give them as a housewarming gift for a friend who is moving.

➤ To give the placemats extra interest, use a novelty yarn for the contrasting color.

➤ For a different look, crochet the mat using one color, and weave across all strands using a second color.

The Least You Need to Know

➤ You can use techniques you've learned and apply them in new and exciting ways.

➤ Crochet is very flexible and allows you to embellish it using different techniques such as weaving.

➤ You can make fringe by tying together woven strands, rather than adding a new tuft of yarn.

Part 5
Final Helps

You've knitted like the dickens and crocheted up a storm. Is your piece complete? Probably not. It's now time to sew together and block. In this section, you'll learn all the professional tricks for completing your pieces.

In addition, because you'll want to share your newfound skills with your family and friends, I'll go over a few gift-giving basics: when to give, what to give, and when to keep it to yourself.

Chapter 24

Finishing Your Work

In This Chapter

➤ Common finishing abbreviations

➤ The stellar selvage stitch

➤ Working through your seaming options

➤ Blocking to make your piece shape up

➤ A couple decorative crochet edges to add a fun touch

Nothing—absolutely nothing—can sabotage your hard work knitting and crochet like a bad finishing job. You might spend months knitting a complex Fair Isle sweater, but if the seams are sloppy and the piece isn't blocked into shape, the results will be mediocre at best.

Many knitters and crocheters skimp on the finishing touches. Don't. The extra time you spend making your pieces look truly professional will be worth the effort.

In this chapter, you'll learn how to professionally seam and block a piece. You'll also learn about some simple edgings that are fun to work and attractive to look at. So let's get started!

Common Abbreviations

The following universal abbreviations will come in handy when you're finishing your work. For a full list of knit and crochet abbreviations, see the tearcard at the front of this book.

Abbreviation...	What It Means...
fin	Finished
in(s)	Inch(es)
kwise	Knit-wise
pc	Picot crochet
pwise	Purl-wise
rem	Remaining
rs	Right side
sc	Single crochet
sl	Slip
sl st	Slip stitch
ws	Wrong side

For Knitters Only—Creating Selvage Edges

You can actually add a finishing touch to your work *as* you knit by working a selvage stitch. These stitches produce a noncurling edge that provides a clean basis for sewing seams or adding neck ribbing. In fact, some pattern directions—such as those for shawls, scarves, and afghans— instruct you to work the first stitch of each row in a selvage stitch.

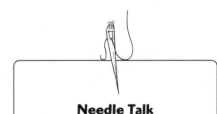

Needle Talk

A *slip stitch* is a stitch that is moved from one needle to the other without being worked. When a pattern instructs you to *slip a stitch knit-wise* or *slip a stitch purl-wise*, insert the needle into the stitch as though you were going to knit or purl the stitch. Now just slip that stitch, unworked, off the left needle and onto the right needle.

Here's how you make the simple *chain-edge selvage* on a stockinette stitched piece:

Row 1 (right side): Slip the first stitch knit-wise; work across the row; knit the last stitch in the row.

Row 2 (wrong side): Slip the first stitch purl-wise; work across the row; purl the last stitch in the row.

Work these two rows through the entire piece. You'll end up with clean, noncurling edges composed of chain-like stitches.

Another useful selvage stitch is the *slipped garter edge*. This stitch is decorative, making it ideal for edges that can stand alone. Here's how:

On every row, slip the first stitch knit-wise and knit the last stitch.

See? This selvage is very easy—and easy to remember because you do the same thing on each row.

Sewing Up the Seams

Imagine a world-class chef assembling the makings of a wonderful meal: imported truffles, free-range chicken breasts, spices found only in the tiny herb shop on Fifth Avenue. The chef carefully simmers the meal, sets out the Spode, meticulously tastes and re-tastes the sauce. All the love he has for food is poured into these preparations.

And then, moments before he is to serve a culinary delight never before experienced, he runs out of patience, turns up the stovetop, and boils every smidgen of flavor from the meal until he ends with something the worst chain restaurant wouldn't dream of serving.

Have I made my point? All the work and time you put into knitting and crocheting pieces mean that those pieces deserve your care and attention at the end of the project—when it comes time to piece them together. If you're feeling impatient, go work on something else for a while. Never give your finishing work short shrift.

This section covers the many methods available for joining pieces. Complete this step carefully and thoughtfully, and don't be afraid to pull out the seams and rework them if they look uneven.

To piece together your work, you'll need a yarn needle and, depending on the method you choose, a crochet hook. You'll also need some straight pins to hold the seams while you're joining them.

Snarls

Proceed with caution if you plan to work selvage stitches in a pattern that doesn't call for them—especially a pattern that has a fancy knit/purl combination stitch across the piece. If you don't add *extra stitches for selvages*, your pattern won't work out correctly across the rows, which will affect all shaping.

Pointers

To assemble pieces, lie them on a flat surface and gently stretch them so that they match through the seam. Pin the beginning and end of the seam. Now align the pieces at the center of the seam, and pin this area. Continue matching and pinning until the seam is completely pinned—with pins approximately 1" to 2" apart. If you are seaming a piece in which the front and back have a matching stitch pattern—such as a cable-knit sweater—match these patterns carefully. Also, be sure to pin the *right* sides together so that the seam is on the inside.

Backstitching

Backstitching is a means of hand sewing your pieces together. As you might guess, you'll need a yarn needle to backstitch. Backstitching provides a fairly elastic, flexible seam that is also sturdy. For this reason, it's great for curved edges and delicate pieces.

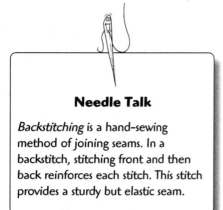

> ### Needle Talk
>
> *Backstitching* is a hand-sewing method of joining seams. In a backstitch, stitching front and then back reinforces each stitch. This stitch provides a sturdy but elastic seam.

To backstitch, use the same yarn you used to knit or crochet the piece. Insert the needle into the beginning of the seam, about a half-stitch in from the side selvage. Now insert the needle about 2 stitches down the seam from the original position. Count back 1 stitch and reinsert the needle. Count forward 2 stitches and reinsert the needle. Count back 2 stitches and reinsert the needle. Continue in this method all the way down the seam.

When you backstitch, be sure that the stitches are close enough together to prevent the seam from gaping or leaving holes that can pull open. If you can see holes in the seam, you've probably created stitches that are too large and you will need to pull out and redo the seam.

Backstitching a knitted piece.

Backstitching a crocheted piece.

Pointers

You determine the size yarn needle you need by the weight of the yarn with which you're sewing. You need to be able to thread the yarn through the eye of the needle. Because you'll no doubt be working with different weights of yarn in your knitting and crocheting career, next time you feel like treating yourself, why not pick up some yarn needles in different sizes?

Overcast or Whip Stitching Together

Overcast or *whip stitching*, also worked with a yarn needle, is a great way to join squares or strips together. Just as its name implies, you are "whipping" your pieces together. This produces an effect inside the seam that looks a lot like the vests cowboys wear in western movies.

To whipstitch, insert your needle, back to front, working over the last stitch only on each piece. Repeat this process, being careful not to pull the yarn too tight.

Whipstitching a knitted piece.

241

Whipstitching a crocheted piece.

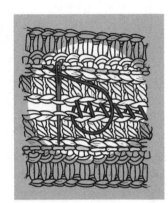

You can create a decorative effect by whipping together the two front loops of the pattern stitch.

Pointers

You can create some interesting and decorative effects by whipstitching in a color that contrasts the pieces you're sewing. In these cases, the whipstitching is to be on the outside, so you need to pin the *wrong* sides of the pieces together.

Slip Stitching Together

Put down the yarn needle. This next seaming technique requires a crochet hook. *Slip stitching* a seam together creates a very firm, even edge that works well for straight seams. If you make a mistake, you can easily remove the seam pulling back the slip stitches. Because this seaming method can produce a fairly inflexible seam, it's not great for curved areas such as armholes.

To slip stitch a seam, attach the yarn to the two outer loops of your pattern stitch. Now slip stitch in every stitch of the seam. (If you need a little extra slip-stitch help, turn to Chapter 17.)

Check your seam often to be sure that it's not puckering. If the fabric is being pulled into the seam, rip out the seam and slip stitch more loosely; the seam needs to lie flat. A slip stitched seam can get bulky if you're not careful. To cut down on extra bulk, only stitch through one loop of every stitch, rather than both loops.

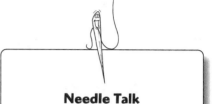

Needle Talk

Slip stitch seaming is joining two pieces of work together with yarn and a crochet hook. This technique produces a strong, tight join that works well on flat seams.

Slip stitching a seam on a knitted piece.

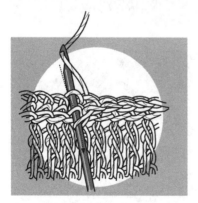

Slip stitching a seam on a crocheted piece.

Weaving Together Seams and Ends

Weaving together is the most inconspicuous of all methods of joining. In weaving, you are butting the two pieces together rather than sewing a seam from the selvage. As a result, the piece has no visible seams.

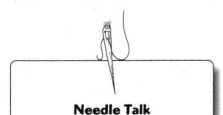

Needle Talk

Weaving is a finishing method in which pieces are butted together, a join is worked on the right side of the piece, and no visible seam appears.

You weave on the *right* side of your work using a yarn needle. Be careful to match the rows when you put your pieces together. To weave, you'll need a yarn needle and the same yarn you used on the project.

With the two pieces laying flat and the right sides facing up, insert the needle into the first half of the stitch on the left-hand side. Pass the needle from the front to the back on the right-hand corresponding stitch; you now come back up on the right-hand side. Continue this process all the way up the seam.

The seam should remain flat. If you notice it puckering, pull out the stitches and rework the seam with a looser hand.

Weaving a seam on a knitted piece.

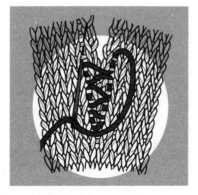

Weaving a seam on a crocheted piece.

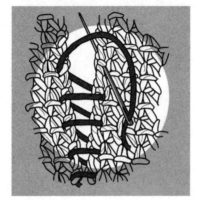

For Knitters Only: Grafting

Knitters have one final option not open to crocheters: *grafting*. Also called the *kitchener stitch*, this clever little stitch enables you to, essentially, create a knitted row using a yarn needle. You can then join together active stitches, provided the two pieces you're joining have the same number of active stitches.

You can use grafting to create a nearly invisible seam at the shoulders of sweaters, the ends of socks, and the tips of mittens.

This stitch is a little tricky initially. Just follow the instructions to the letter and you'll be fine.

1. Cut the active yarn (the yarn currently feeding from the end of your work) with a tail about 1¹/₂″ long for every stitch you'll be grafting. Thread this yarn through a yarn needle.

2. With the 2 rows of stitches to be joined, align the wrong sides of the stitches together.

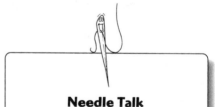

Needle Talk

Grafting or *kitchener stitch* is a means of joining two active rows of knitting so that the join resembles a row of knitted stitches.

Insert the yarn needle, as if to knit, through the first stitch on the front needle. Slip this stitch off the knitting needle.

Insert the yarn needle, as if to purl, through the next stitch on the needle in front. Leave this stitch on the knitting needle.

Insert the yarn needle, as if to purl, through the first stitch on the back needle. Slip this stitch off the knitting needle.

245

3. Insert the yarn needle, as if to knit, through the next stitch on the back needle. Leave this stitch on the knitting needle.

4. Repeat these steps—beginning with step 2, working through the illustrations, and ending with step 3—until you have only 1 stitch remaining. Draw the yarn through this stitch and secure it on the wrong side.

Grafting creates a seam that resembles a knitted row.

Final Call: Weaving in Yarn Tails

By the time you finish a piece, you'll find you have lots of small yarn tails that need attention. To hide them, you *weave in* the ends. Begin with a yarn needle or a small crochet hook. Now use the needle or hook to work the ends into the wrong side of the fabric. Using the needle, pull the yarn through, making sure that it doesn't show from the right side. Now, using sharp scissors, snip the ends of the yarn, taking special care not to cut through the fabric.

Using a yarn needle to weave in yarn tails on a knitted piece.

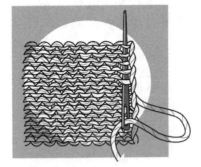

Using a crochet hook to weave in yarn tails on a crocheted piece.

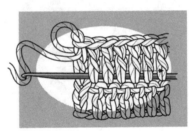

246

Blocking

After you finish seaming a piece, you might look at it and be mildly disappointed. It's not that the seams don't lie flat. They do. It's just that, somehow, the piece seems a little warbly. A little out of shape. Here's where blocking comes in.

Blocking is one of the easiest-to-execute and most often–neglected steps in knitting and crocheting. I admit I always skipped this step. "Too complex!" I exclaimed. Nonsense. Blocking is very easy and rewarding. It's also somewhat addicting once you see what a metamorphosis your piece undergoes during this final step.

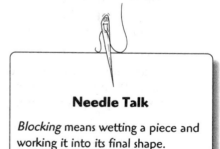

Needle Talk

Blocking means wetting a piece and working it into its final shape.

Wet Blocking

To start, first prepare a surface on which you'll leave the item to dry. Your bed is a good choice. Or a spot on the floor that will get little foot traffic. Get almost every towel you have in the house; you'll need lots. Lay down a couple thicknesses of towels on the area; the towel area should be slightly larger than the item you're blocking.

Begin by filling the sink with lukewarm water. If the temperature is significantly different from the room temperature, you could scare some fibers into reacting crazily: shrinking or felting or pilling.

Gently submerge the knitted or crocheted item into the water. If the piece is made of wool, you might have to gently work it up and down to wet it; wool has natural water-repellent properties.

Pointers

Blocking is an integral step for shaping fitted pieces such as sweaters and socks. It's also wonderful for shaping wool blankets and pillow tops. If, however, you're making an acrylic or machine-washable and –dryable cotton afghan, blanket, or pillow top, don't bother blocking. Throw the item in the washer and dryer. It'll actually come out fluffier and cozier than if you blocked it.

When the item is wetted down, let the water out of the sink, and very gently press down on the item to squeeze out some excess water.

Lay down a couple towels next to the sink, lay the item on these, and roll up the towels. Gently press down on the towels to get rid of excess water. The towels might now be soaked. You might need to lay down another set of towels and repeat the rolling and squeezing process.

Now lay out the item on the prepared surface. Get out your measuring tape and use it to determine how wide and long the piece should be. Gently stretch the piece into this size. Match up all the seams. Run your hands gently over the piece to smooth it flat; you are essentially "ironing" the piece with your hands. Wait a while.

Come back in about an hour and, if necessary, place dry towels under the piece. Keep doing this until the piece is dry. It'll be wonderfully shaped, with flat seams, ready to use.

The Pinning Method

The pinning method requires a lot more pins and a lot less water than the wet-blocking method.

To begin, you need to prepare a surface. You'll be pinning the finished piece to this surface and then wetting down the piece. If the piece is small, you can fold two towels in half and stack them on top of each other (to create a surface four towels thick). If the piece is larger, you'll need to wrap a towel over a piece of board, such as plywood.

After you've prepared the surface, pin the piece to the surface using the measurements given in the pattern for the finished piece. For example, if a sweater should be 23 inches long from the shoulder to the bottom, measure and pin it at 23 inches long.

Measure and pin the length of the piece. Then measure and pin the width. Then measure and pin rounded or irregular areas such as the neckline. Finally, pin any edges that are rolling.

Measure and pin a piece to prepare it for blocking.

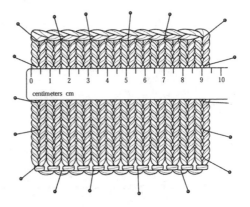

Now either spritz the piece gently with water, or lay wet towels on it. Then wait a while. When the water dries, unpin the piece. The seams will be flat and the piece will be in its finished shape.

A Final Bonus: Crocheted Edges

Crocheted edgings can add a special touch to knitted or crocheted items. Let's play around with a couple; you'll want to keep these little gems in your bag of tricks to pull out when you need to add a special zing to a piece. Edgings are usually started on the right side, and you can generally plan on working one edge stitch into each stitch of the knitted or crocheted piece.

Slip Stitch Edging

Slip stitch edging is an easy stitch that leaves an attractive, firm edge. You can use this edging as an accent in a different color from the main piece, or as a finishing edge in the same color as the main piece. To work this edging, follow the same procedure you learned in Chapter 17 for slip stitching.

Pointers

Keep your work flat when you are adding edging. Otherwise, the piece will pucker into the edging, ruining the effect. To ensure flatness, you might even want to work the edging with the piece resting on a table rather than in your lap. If you are working around corners, work 3 stitches into each corner so that the corners will remain firm squares.

Reverse single crochet adds a braid-like edge to your pieces.

Reverse Single Crochet Edging

If you've read Chapters 17 and 22, you're very familiar with working a single crochet stitch. Now try working a *reverse* single crochet edging. Instead of working from right to left, you'll be working from left to right.

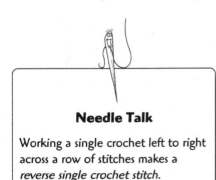

Reverse single crochet gives you the look of a braided edge. This step can be a little rough initially; practice for a bit to get all your stitches even.

Here are easy instructions for working reverse single crochet:

1. Attach your yarn to a stitch on the left side of your work and pull up a loop.

2. Moving from left to right, insert your hook into the next stitch and again pull up a loop. Yarn over the hook to complete the single crochet.

3. Continue steps 1 and 2 to complete the edge.

> **Needle Talk**
>
> Working a single crochet left to right across a row of stitches makes a *reverse single crochet stitch.*

To create a slip stitched edge, insert your crochet hook into the top of a stitch and pull up a loop.

When you come to corners, complete as many reverse stitches as are necessary to keep the corners sharp and flat. Three reverse single crochets to each corner is a good rule of thumb.

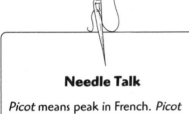

> **Needle Talk**
>
> *Picot* means peak in French. *Picot edging* is a decorative stitch that features little points of crochet.

Picot Edging

Picot is another very distinctive edging. It offers a lacy look that is wonderful for finishing baby projects and doilies, and it makes a great alternative to fringe on a shawl.

Picots, formed with 3, 4, or 5 chains can be made on top of most stitches. Here's how to make a 3-chain picot edge formed with single crochet; to work a 4- or 5-chain picot, simply make 4 or 5 chains in the first step:

1. With the right side of the work facing you, attach the yarn, work 3 single crochets, and then chain 3.

2. Repeat step 1 across the edge.

The Least You Need to Know

➤ Using selvage stitch while knitting can prepare edges to be seamed.

➤ Take your time when finishing your piece; a bad finishing job can negate all your hard knitting and crocheting work.

➤ Blocking pieces shapes them up and gives them a professional look.

➤ You can add decorative crocheted edges to either knitted or crocheted pieces.

Chapter 25

Worthy Recipients: A Couple Thoughts on Giving Away Your Projects

---

In This Chapter

➤ Making your gift list and checking it twice

➤ Creating gifts that others will love

➤ Adding yourself to the gift list

By now you have a raft of skills that enable you to knit and crochet to your heart's content. No doubt you're going to want to use your new crafts to create beautiful things for your friends and family.

But, at some point, it'll happen. You'll spend every free moment working a unique gift for someone you care about, running through in your mind the tearful scene when the recipient rips open the package and praises your thoughtfulness, your workmanship, your contribution to bettering life as we know it…

And when the package is actually opened, you receive a noncommittal, "Wow. A scarf. Hey, thanks." Or you spend months stitching a beautiful merino shawl for your sister only to find it at the bottom of her drawer, and she claims she isn't really a shawl person or that wool makes her skin itch.

I know the scene well; I've lived it many times, as have hundreds of other knitters and crocheters. It's heartbreaking to spend free time working a "perfect" gift for a friend only to find that he would rather have a gift certificate to the Sharper Image. This chapter is filled with the advice of other stitchers: how to make gifts that others will appreciate, how to choose the members of your gift list, and when to stop treating others and start treating yourself. Read on.

Choosing Your Gift List

Handcrafting a piece is time consuming and, sometimes, painstaking. A handmade sweater or afghan represents not only the item itself, but also the gift of hours of your time. Some people understand what you're giving them; others simply see another sweater, not unlike the one they saw in a mail-order catalog last week.

After talking with dozens of knitters and crocheters, one piece of advice came through loud and clear:

Don't try to convert the unconvertible.

Just as it's next to impossible to make a natural spendthrift frugal, so is it nearly insurmountable to make someone appreciate your handiwork who doesn't understand what the gift represents. Limit your list to those people who will love not only what you've made for them, but also appreciate the gift of your time and thoughts while stitching it.

Pointers

If you want to stitch for others but don't have enough appreciative friends or family members to absorb all your output, consider knitting or crocheting for charity. Homeless shelters always welcome caps, mittens, and scarves. Shelters for abused women or teenage mothers appreciate and put to good use any baby or toddler items you make. One favorite, quick, and beautiful pattern that makes a lovely charity gift is the five-hour baby sweater. (You'll need some experience to make this sweater.) You can find the pattern on the Internet at http://www.woolworks.org/patterns/5-hour.txt.

Your time is too precious, your work too stunning, to waste it trying to win over those who can't appreciate what you're doing. Buy them something from the mall and save your labors for yourself and a small list of family members and friends who truly appreciate and understand what you're doing.

Making Gifts Others Will Love

In all fairness, some people don't love handmade gifts not because they're unapprecia-tive boors, but because, well, the gifts look unattractively homemade. All of us have had a well-meaning great-aunt who's whipped up a bumper crop of frilly acrylic crocheted aprons to fit over dish detergent bottles. Does it mean you don't appreciate her efforts because you prefer not to dress household cleaning products? No. Sometimes the problem truly *is* with the gift and not the recipient.

The tips in this section should help you direct your efforts toward gifts that others will love.

Limit Your List

An added benefit to choosing your gift list wisely is that you can make a more concentrated effort to dazzling those few people who make the cut. Rather than make a slew of crocheted tissue-paper covers for 20 of your closest friends, you can work a crocheted lace shawl for your mother or a Fair Isle sweater for your best friend.

Use High-Quality Fibers

If you're going to spend the time and effort and care to make gifts for people you love, choose the best fiber you can. Instead of working up an acrylic vest, why not try mohair? Or heather wool? Or a comfy nubby cotton?

One added bonus to using high-quality fibers is that they can camouflage your beginning-level skills. A plain single-crocheted lap throw is classic looking in undyed wool. A simple stockinette stitch baby sweater looks ready for the boutique in a funky boucle yarn.

Make Universally Welcome Gifts

If you're stitching for people who appreciate your effort but are still very particular, stick to gifts everyone likes or can use: those that don't have to be displayed in a home or publicly on a person. For example, a set of crocheted dishcloths bundled with some flavored vinegars is universally usable; everyone has to wash dishes and wipe up the counters. Likewise, almost everyone can use soft rag wool socks for keeping feet warm while lingering over the Sunday-morning paper.

Pointers

The guideline of not making wearable gifts for pickier recipients has one notable exception: parents of babies. Few mothers or fathers won't welcome a handmade sweater set for a newborn. In addition, tiny baby sweaters, hats, and blankets are a good way to use up leftover yarn from larger projects.

Don't Insist on the Element of Surprise

Nothing can dampen your spirits more than presenting a handmade gift with great pomp and ceremony, only to receive a lukewarm response. The response might be the result of a bad day, but most generally it's because the style, yarn, or color doesn't suit the recipient. It's disappointing to buy someone a gift and find that you missed the mark, but the blow is much more severe when you've labored for months to find that not only is the gift off target—and nonreturnable.

Rather than trying to surprise someone with a gift featuring your newfound knitting and crocheting skills, why not involve that person in the process? If you really want to make a sweater for your choosy husband, let him select the color, style, and type of yarn. You're still giving a wonderful gift, but this time you're making something you *know* he'll love.

The only downside to involving a recipient is the potential for constant nagging regarding when the gift will be finished. If you involve the receiver in a gift selection, be sure to stress that your *goal* is to finish it by a certain date, but situations could prevent you from doing so. Nothing can kill the joy of knitting and crocheting like deadline pressure.

The Virtue of Selfishness

For some reason, knitters and crocheters, on the whole, seem to be selfless to a fault. They believe that the joy they receive from crafting and working with beautiful fibers should be reward enough, and the fruits of their labor should go elsewhere. The concept is perplexing. After all, amateur photographers don't feel like they need to give away all their lenses. Stereophiles don't feel guilty if they're not giving friends high-powered receivers.

Likewise, you should always feel comfortable enjoying your work. If you want to try making a lace tablecloth or an intricately patterned cable sweater, remember that you don't *have* to find a recipient. Instead, you *can* make something wonderful for yourself. If your friends and family members would rather have store-bought items, buy their gifts at a department store and use your knitting and crocheting energy to make yourself happy.

Pointers

Never let knitting and crocheting become a chore. This is a hobby, a craft, a way to unwind in a world that would have you wound tightly 24 hours a day. Never let perceived duty or guilt rob you of the fun of stitching and the pleasure of creating. You don't "owe" anyone handcrafted gifts. Give only to those who understand the significance of your stitching, and take pleasure in making exquisite pieces for yourself.

The Least You Need to Know

➤ You can't teach others to appreciate your knitting and crocheting; don't try.

➤ Always use high-quality fibers and styles suitable for the recipient when giving handcrafted gifts.

➤ If you're stitching for a choosy recipient, involve her in the process of selecting the pattern, yarn, and color.

➤ Never feel guilty about making something wonderful for yourself. You, better than anyone, will appreciate the work and craftsmanship of your pieces.

Resource Guide

This appendix lists books, magazines, and suppliers you might find helpful as you begin knitting and crocheting. Most of these are simply my favorites—or my favorites that are still in print. To find more, check your library, bookstore, and the Internet.

Books

The Crochet Collection
Leisure Arts
ISBN: 0-942237-55-2
$14.95
Neat, fun projects to wear and use around the house.

Elizabeth Zimmermann's Knitter's Almanac
Elizabeth Zimmermann
Dover Publications, Inc.
ISBN: 0-486-24178-5
$5.95
My favorite of the Elizabeth Zimmermann titles, this tiny, inexpensive book includes projects for each month of the year, with valuable tips and tricks.

The Filet Crochet Book
Chris Rankin
Lark Books
ISBN: 0-80693-823-5
$16.95
A wonderful book full of filet crochet patterns and techniques.

Glorious Crocheted Sweaters
Nola Theiss, Editor
Sterling Publishing Company
ISBN: 0-8069-6991-1
$14.95
This book puts to rest any notions that crocheted sweaters need to look dowdy and old-fashioned. The sweaters in this collection are stunning.

Gorgeous Crochet Laces for Interior Decoration
Ondori/Japan Publications
ISBN: 0-87040-487-3
$17
Beautiful and delicate lace patterns to try.

The Harmony Guides: 300 Crochet Stitches, Volume 6
Trafalgar Square
ISBN: 1-855-85634-4
$15.95
A wealth of crochet patterns to play with: lace, motifs, shells, filet, bobbles, and loops.

The Harmony Guide to Aran and Fair Isle Knitting
Debra Mountford, Editor
Crown Trade Paperbacks
ISBN: 0-517-88405-4
$17
A great explanation of Fair Isle and Aran techniques, along with a glossary of pattern stitches.

Knitting in America
Melanie D. Falick
Artisan
ISBN: 1-885183-27-5
$35
A truly inspiring book and the best American knitting book to come out in years; profiles more than 30 American artisans and includes original patterns.

The New Knitting Stitch Library
Lesley Stanfield
Lark Books
ISBN: 1-57990-027-5
$21.95
A solid glossary of knitting stitches with stitches appropriate for all expertise levels of knitters.

Quick and Cozy Afghans
Leisure Arts
ISBN: 0-942237-48-X
$14.95
A nice collection of crocheted afghans. The expertise levels range from beginner to advanced, so you can use this book all through your crocheting life.

Slip-Stitch Knitting: Color Pattern the Easy Way
Roxana Bartlett
Interweave Press
ISBN: 1-883010-32-2
$21.95
Explains an interesting and easy method for adding color to knitting through striping colors and strategically slipping stitches.

Vanna's Afghans A to Z: 52 Crochet Favorites
Vanna White; Nancy J. Fitzpatrick, Editor
Oxmoor House
ISBN: 0848714768
$14.95
A fun concept: Vanna White takes you through the alphabet with cleverly named afghans. Some of the patterns are real keepers.

A Treasury of Knitting Patterns
Barbara Walker
Schoolhouse Press
ISBN: 0942018168
$30

A Second Treasury of Knitting Patterns
Barbara Walker
Schoolhouse Press
ISBN: 0942018176
$30

A Third Treasury of Knitting Patterns
Barbara Walker
Schoolhouse Press
$30
ISBN: 0942018184
These three classic books have just been re-released by Schoolhouse Press and are must-haves for serious knitters looking for stitch patterns.

Periodicals

Interweave Knits
201 East Fourth Street
Loveland, CO 80537-5655
(970) 669–7672
http://www.interweave.com
$24 U.S. ($31 Canada) for a one-year subscription or $42 U.S. ($56 Canada) for a two-year subscription. Published four times per year.
Solid knitting patterns and interesting feature articles.

Knitter's
XRX, Inc.
824 West 10th Street
Sioux Falls, SD 57104-3518
(605) 338–2450

www.xrx-inc.com
$16 U.S. ($30 Canada) for one-year subscription; $20 U.S. ($38 Canada) for a two-year subscription. Published four times per year.
A great magazine for all levels of expertise; many patterns per issue and some good technique articles.

Knitting Digest
P.O. Box 9002
Big Sandy, TX 75755
(800) 829–5865
$14.95 U.S. ($22.95 Canada) for a one-year subscription. Published bimonthly.
A more traditional knitting magazine; smaller trim size, patterns are less modern than you will find in Knitter's *or* Vogue Knitting, *but an appealing format.*

Piecework
201 East Fourth Street
Loveland, CO 80537-5655
(970) 669–7672
http://www.interweave.com
$24 U.S. ($31 Canada) for a one-year subscription. Published bimonthly.
A compendium of crafts from a historical perspective. Often contains knitting and crocheting articles.

Vogue Knitting
P.O. Box 1072
Altoona, PA 16603
(800) 289–4304
$11.95 U.S. ($16.50 Canada) for a one-year subscription. Published three times per year (March, August, October).
The perfect magazine for knitters who want to wear Versace and Calvin Klein, but don't want to pay the price; good patterns for all expertise levels.

Woolgathering
Schoolhouse Press
Pittsville, WI 54466
(800) YOU–KNIT
$20 U.S. for a three-year subscription. Published twice per year (March, September).
A legendary newsletter started by Elizabeth Zimmermann and now run by Meg Swansen.

Yarn and Tools

Bernat
P.O. Box 435
Lockport, NY 14094
www.bernat.com/index.html
Great selection of lower-priced yarns. This is the company that makes both Sugar 'n Cream and Handicrafter cotton yarns, two great yarns for dishcloths and facecloths.

Brittany
P.O. Box 130
Dept. P
Elk, CA 95432
(888) 488–9669
Wonderful fine wood knitting needles and crochet hooks. Brittany also makes a great three-pack of wooden cable needles in varying sizes.

Brown Sheep Yarn Company
100662 County Road 16
Mitchell, NE 69357
(308) 635–2189
Good, reasonably priced yarns in natural fibers as well as attractive, classic patterns.

Classic Elite Yarns
12 Perkins Street
Lowell, MA 01854
(508) 453–2837
Beautiful yarns in mostly natural fibers and wonderful knitting patterns. Classic Elite also puts out some kits to make socks, hats, gloves, and bags.

Coats & Clark
P.O. Box 27067
Greenville, SC 29616
(864) 234–0331
(800) 648–1479
www.coatsandclark.com
A great resource for crochet cotton, an instructional crochet video, and knitting and crochet tools.

Lion Brand Yarn Company
34 West 15th Street
New York, NY 10011
(800) 258–YARN (9276)
www.lionbrand.com
Nice selection of moderately priced yarns. Some natural fibers, although most are synthetic or synthetic blends. Makes a wonderful fisherman's wool that comes in 8-ounce skeins.

Morehouse Farm
RD 2, Box 408
Red Hook, NY 12571
(914) 758–6493
Soft merino wool made from the sheep on this farm. If you're in the area, stop by. If you're in New York City, visit the booth at the Union Square Farmer's Market Mondays and Wednesdays.

Patternworks
P.O. Box 1690
Poughkeepsie, NY 12601
(800) 438–5464
http://www.patternworks.com
A great source for yarn and knitting and crochet tools, as well as patterns, kits, and accessories. Write or call for a catalog.

School Products Company, Inc.
1201 Broadway
New York, NY 10001
(212) 679–3516
(800) 847–4127
http://www.schoolproducts.com
A great source for patterns, supplies, and bulk yarn. Because of the fluctuations of stocking, available yarn colors can vary.

Schoolhouse Press
6899 Cary Bluff
Pittsville, WI 54466
(800) YOU–KNIT
Beautiful, one-of-a-kind yarns and intriguing patterns. Started by knitting legend Elizabeth Zimmermann and now run by her daughter, second-generation knitting legend Meg Swansen.

Sheep Stuff/Michigan Farm Woolies
Mt. Bruce Station
6440 Bordman Road
Romeo, MI 48065
(810) 798–2568
uhlianuk@sheepstuff.com
www.sheepstuff.com
Beautiful naturally dyed yarns spun from the sheep on this farm. Custom-designed hand-knit items are also available, if you're feeling more like wearing than making.

Webs
P.O. Box 147
Northampton, MA 01061-0147
(800) FOR–WEBS (367–9327)
www.yarn.com
Great, inexpensive resource for bulk yarn. Fine supplier for knitting and crochet tools, patterns, and books.

Glossary of Terms

Afghan crochet A special type of crochet that requires the crocheter to hold many stitches on the crochet hook. Special afghan hooks that look like a cross between a crochet hook and a knitting needle are available for this purpose. Also called *Tunisian crochet.*

back-post double crochet (bpdc) A special crochet stitch that involves working into the back of the post of a crochet stitch on the row.

backstitching A hand-sewing method of joining seams. In a backstitch, stitching front and then back reinforces each stitch. This stitch provides a sturdy but elastic seam.

binding off The process in which you "lock up" all active stitches on the needle so that they can't unravel. You bind off stitches when you're finished with a piece or want to shape an area—such as an armhole in a sweater.

blocking A means of wetting a piece and working it into its final shape.

bobbins Plastic tabs that hold small amounts of yarn. Bobbins are invaluable when working on pieces that have many color changes.

bottom selvage The cast-on row in knitting.

cable needles Small double-pointed needles made expressly for creating patterned cables, such as those on Aran sweaters.

cable panel The stockinette stitch column on which a cable is worked.

cables Specialized knitting patterns created by physically moving stitches and knitting them out of their original order.

casting on The process of creating the foundation row of stitches from which you will knit.

chain stitch (ch st) A crochet stitch made by catching the yarn with the crochet hook and drawing the yarn through the loop on the hook.

closing a stitch   The step in crochet in which a stitch is finished and only one loop remains on the crochet hook. When changing colors, you always close the last stitch of the current color with the new color.

cluster stitches   Groups of crocheted stitches that give the appearance of a single stitch.

Continental knitting   A type of knitting in which you "catch" the yarn using the needle; you don't use your hand to drape or throw the yarn over the needle.

contrasting color (cc)   An accent color used in a piece. You may have more than one contrasting color.

crochet   A French word meaning "hook." The craft of crochet involves using a hook to join loops of yarn into a fabric.

decrease (dec)   Subtracting the number of active stitches in your work.

double crochet (dc)   A versatile, tall crochet stitch. To make the double crochet stitch, begin with a yarn over; insert the hook into a stitch; yarn over and pull through loop; yarn over and pull through 2 loops; yarn over, and pull through the remaining loops.

double crochet decrease (dec 1 dc)   A crochet stitch that subtracts 1 stitch by combining 2 double crochets.

dropped stitches   Stitches that accidentally came off the needle during knitting. If left unfixed, dropped stitches can run down through the knitted fabric.

duplicate stitch   A needlework technique in which you embroider over knit stitches. The result is a color pattern that appears to be knit in, but is actually embroidered.

dye lot   An indicator of the time the yarn was dyed. Different dye lots—even in the same color yarn—have slight variations in tone if they are dyed at different times.

Fair Isle knitting   A form of knitting in which two colors are used per row, and the color not in use is carried or stranded along the wrong side of the piece.

Kaffe Fassett (pronounced like *safe asset*)   A designer who revolutionized the world of knitting with his colorful, fun, and sometimes outrageous patterns.

filet crochet   A type of crochet in which a pattern is created in the crocheting by arranging blocks and spaces.

foundation chain   A chain-stitched row that stands as the base of all crocheting—the foundation from which a piece is built.

front-post double crochet (fpdc)   A special crochet stitch that involves working into the front of the post of a crochet stitch on the row below.

garter stitch   A common pattern created by knitting every row; it has a fairly bumpy surface.

gauge   The number of stitches you need to complete to finish a specified length of knitted or crocheted fabric. Gauge is typically measured by the inch.

gauge counter   A tool for measuring gauge. To use one, lay the counter over your knitting or crocheting and count the number of stitches that appear in the window.

grafting   A means of joining 2 active rows of knitting so that the join resembles a row of knitted stitches. Also called *Kitchener stitch*.

half-double crochet (hdc)   A cross between a single crochet stitch and a double crochet stitch. To complete a half-double crochet stitch, begin with a yarn over; insert the hook into a stitch; yarn over and pull through the stitch; do another yarn over; and pull through the three loops on your hook.

increase (inc)   Adding more stitches to your work.

Intarsia   A type of color knitting in which each block of color is knit from a separate ball or bobbin of yarn.

Kitchener stitch   See *grafting*.

knitting (k)   Forming rows of interconnecting loops in which the ends of the loops face away from you as you work.

lacet   A special type of mesh in filet crochet that is made by using a single crochet rather than a double or triple crochet. A lacet creates a soft, slightly rounded space.

main color (mc)   The predominant color in a multicolor piece.

mesh   The background of filet crochet; mesh is made up of double or triple crochet stitches separated by a chain or chains.

motifs   Pieces worked around a central point rather than back and forth. Doilies and Granny Squares are two examples of motifs.

picot   A French word meaning *peak*.

picot edging   A decorative stitch that features little points of crochet.

purling (p)   Forming rows of interconnecting loops in which the ends of the loops face away from you as you work.

reverse single crochet stitch   An edging stitch made by working a single crochet left to right, rather than right to left, across a row of stitches.

ribbing   A stitch made by combining knit and purl stitches to form an elastic fabric. Ribbing often begins and ends sweater projects, as well as hats, mittens, and socks.

ridges   The bumps you see on both sides of garter-stitch fabric. Each ridge represents two rows of knitting.

right side (rs)   The side that will be showing on a knitted or crocheted item, such as the outside of a sweater.

ripping out   Unraveling or pulling out stitches. You rip out when you find that you don't like the look or size of the knitted fabric, or when you find a mistake that you need to undo.

single crochet (sc)   The most basic of crochet stitches. To complete a single crochet stitch, insert the hook through a chain (or stitch); yarn over; pull the loop through the chain (or stitch); yarn over again; and pull through both loops on the hook.

single crochet decrease (1 sc dec)   A crochet stitch that subtracts 1 stitch by combining 2 single crochets.

slip knot   A knot that slips easily along the cord around which it is tied. Also called a "running knot."

slip stitch (sl st)   In crochet, a stitch much like a chain stitch except that you create the stitch by working it from a foundation chain or other stitches. In knitting, a stitch that is moved from 1 needle to the other without being worked.

slip stitch seaming   Joining 2 pieces of work together with yarn and a crochet hook. This technique produces a strong, tight join that works well on flat seams.

stash   The inevitable squirreling away of pounds and pounds of yarn a knitter or crocheter doesn't immediately need but might use later.

stitch holders   Safety pin-shaped accessories that hold knitting stitches you aren't currently using but will use later.

stitch markers   Little disks that slide onto your knitting needle or crocheted fabric. Markers cue you at the point when it's time to do something to the fabric, such as increase stitches or begin a new pattern.

stockinette stitch (st st)   A common pattern created by alternating one row of knitting with one row of purling. Stockinette stitch creates a fabric that is smooth on one side and bumpy on the other.

stranding   Carrying the yarn not currently used for a stitch along the back of a piece, ready to be used.

Superwash wool   Specially treated wool that can be safely machine washed.

Meg Swansen   Daughter of Elizabeth Zimmerman, a knitting designer, author, and instructor who runs the knitting-centric Schoolhouse Press.

swatch   A sample you knit or crochet to determine whether or not your gauge is where it should be.

tail   The extra yarn left after you do something in knitting or crocheting, such as casting on a stitch or changing colors.

triple crochet (trc)   A tall crochet stitch. To make this stitch, yarn over the hook twice; insert the hook into a stitch; yarn over and pull through yarn over again and pull through the first 2 loops (the 2 closest to the point); yarn over again and pull through the next 2 loops; yarn over one last time and pull through the remaining 2 loops.

Tunisian crochet   see *Afghan crochet.*

turning chains   Extra chain stitches made at the end of each row to accommodate for the height of the stitch of the next row.

twisted stitches   Stitches twisted on your needle. Because the knitted loops are twisted, the stitches are tighter than correctly knit stitches and don't open when stretched.

twisting   A method of anchoring yarn being carried in the back of your work for more than 5 stitches.

variegated yarn   Yarn dyed with many varying colors—blending from, say, yellow to green to blue.

Barbara Walker   A New Jersey-based writer who added immeasurably to the knitting lexicon by spending more than a decade chronicling hundreds of knitting patterns.

weaving   A finishing method in which pieces are butted together, a join is worked on the right side of the piece, and no visible seam appears.

whipstitch   A technique in which you stitch together a seam by working the tops of the pieces to join.

wrong side (ws)   The side that faces inward in a knitted or crocheted item, such as the inside of a sweater.

yarn over (yo)   In knitting, winding the yarn around a knitting needle to increase one stitch and create a decorative hole in the fabric. In crochet, the movement of passing the hook under the yarn and then catching the yarn with the hook; this movement is fundamental to all crochet stitches.

yarn winder   A funky, two-piece tool that enables you to easily wind skeins of yarn into balls. Generally, only hardcore knitters and crocheters purchase yarn winders.

Elizabeth Zimmermann   A self-proclaimed "opinionated knitter" who promoted knitting for more than 3 decades through her knitting camps, video workshops, *Woolgathering* newsletter, and numerous books.

Index